The Israeli Dilemma

Publications of the Polemological Centre of the
Free University of Brussels (VUB). *Vol. 2*

The Israeli Dilemma
Essays on a Warfare State

Georges R. Tamarin
Director of the Institute for
Socio-Psychological Research, Tel Aviv

Edited by
Johan Niezing
Professor of International Relations and
Director of the Polemological Centre of the
Free University of Brussels (VUB)

1973
Rotterdam University Press

Copyright © 1973 by Universitaire Pers Rotterdam
No part of this book may be reproduced in any form, by print, photoprint, microfilm or any other means without written permission from the publisher.
Printed in the Netherlands

ISBN 90 237 6220 7

Contents

Author's note — VII

Editor's introduction — 1

1. The Israeli dilemma: ghetto state or free society? — 7
2. Legal bases of prejudice and discrimination in Israeli society — 27
3. Non-legal forms of prejudice and discrimination — 51
4. The Israeli authoritarian personality — 77
5. Primitive pollution fears and compulsory premarital ritual — 95
6. Two stereotypes of the national mythology: the Sabra superman and the inferior Diaspora Jew — 113
7. A study in xenophobic associations — 149
8. Patterns of rioting in Israel — 169
9. The influence of ethnic and religious prejudice on moral judgment — 183

Author's note

First, I want to express my sincere gratitude to Professor J. Niezing for selecting and editing the texts comprising this book. Possibly only authors who have been confronted with the arduous problem of condensing a large amount of material into a volume of reasonable size, while safeguarding the basic ideas, can appreciate the magnitude of the task realised.

I also want to thank Professor Niezing and the Rotterdam University Press for endorsing my stand, *not* to rewrite and update in light of later developments, some chapters which were written and/or partly published 6-7 years ago. However, the temptation of 'prophetic hindsight' and of 'accuracy' of ulterior revisions of statements is great indeed and in my opinion scientists should avoid it.

It would be futile to try to point out here the particular changes that took place, pertaining on the one hand but to a few *factual* data, and on the other to recent developments in Israeli social dynamics and values. Futile also since it is questionable whether from the standpoint of *change* one should in *our case* place greater emphasis on those actual phenomena which run *counter* the pre-existing tendencies, or those new minor facts which enhance them, when in the second case it is a question of semantics to what measure one deals with change. For instance, when law-projects, mentioned in the text, aimed at furthering the legalized semi-totalitarian rule of party-bureaucracies and of the rabbinical establishment, they were in the meantime enacted as laws.

Concerning factual changes it is nonetheless indispensable to state that every text dealing with legal aspects of prejudice and discrimination - and with the Jewish identity - has to be supplemented with the historical verdict of the Supreme Court in the (first) Shalit case in 1970, the subsequent theocratic amendment of the 'Law of Return' and 'Law of Registry of Residents', undoing the implications of the liberal ruling, assuring the right also of those half-Jews whose mother is a non-Jewess to be registered as Jews, and the latest hitherto unsuccessful attempts to fight the actual situation by legal action. This includes among others the second Shalit case (1972), mirroring the absurdness of the fact, that while the first two children are registered as Jews, this is refused to the younger son, born after the amendment of the law. Incidentally, this lawsuit, as well as the pending (1972) *order nisi* of the 'black Hebrews', are illustrative of the fact that any attempt to update the material would be hopeless, there is every chance that between writing and publication some relevant new developments *will* occur. This may be the result of some coalitionary dealing, a new immigration wave or change in the military situation; it applies to those aspects of prejudices which are discussed in this book, and also those (i.e. intercommunal antagonisms and Jewish-Arab relations) which remained outside its framework.

The same is true for changes related to social dynamics and ideology, rooted in the developments of (what I termed) the Israeli petite-bourgeoisie revolution and, more recently, the experience and aftermath of the Six Day War. They pertain mostly to a continuing change of those attitudes which were analysed in 'The Israeli Authoritarian Personality'. Fluidity and contradiction characterizes this realm, official myths are still affirmed, but one lives according to a different set of values. This could also express a fundamental paradox of Israeli life, where immobilism and extreme conservatism (reflecting the interests of the ruling old-timer bureaucracy which dominates the institutions) intermingle with incessant changes in some walks of life.

My next remark might sound superfluous given the self-evidence of the statement. Nevertheless in view of the almost pathological oversensitivity of my countrymen, it has to be said that my book is not a description of Israeli society, but of *prejudices* rampant in it (most of the studies were subjects from my courses on prejudice). Thus, *per definitionem* it deals with the dark and negative aspects of Israeli social life and beliefs. Literature dedicated to the sociology of contemporary Israel will have to present a balanced picture of light and shadow, heroism and corruption, progressive achievements and obscurantist setbacks; this however does not impair the legitimacy of publication of studies dealing with the specific subject of prejudices.

By the same token, I have to reject the objection which I encountered time and again, that these findings should not be published since they can be abused by hostile propaganda. *Nothing* can prevent dishonest misinterpretation and propagandistic falsification of scientific data. And, as I have stated this more than once, Israel's most vociferous opponents have the least moral justification for their criticism, since totalitarian denial of human rights and racialist-religious intolerance (even if at times couched in pseudo-revolutionary phraseology) surpass in those countries and movements almost anything which is objectionable in Israeli reality. I can therefore only repeat that as long as this unfortunate planet of ours is divided into anachronistic nation-states, nothing can dispute Israel's right to exist. The more democratic, less prejudiced, exclusive and more open to criticism it becomes, the moral and pragmatic justification of its existence will become more apparent.

In the same context I cannot avoid saying a few words about the 'Tamarin affair' which relates to my investigations and in itself is a symptom of reigning intolerance, which several years ago also received wide coverage in the foreign press. It should however, not be viewed as a *typical* symptom of conditions concerning freedom of expression in Israel. As I wrote recently while explaining some difficulties on research: 'the so-called "Tamarin-affair", which for almost five years preoccupied Israeli academic and public circles, was at least as much an expression of the morality of our 'academic nouveaux riches' as of the stances of the educational authorities. Many of the author's colleagues at the recently established Tel Aviv University were only too eager to comply with the Ministry of Education's demand to discontinue his position, and he is particularly appreciative of the unreserved support of his numerous *political opponents* from the older universities, who assisted him in his fight for academic freedom. Licking of academic and political boots, and supplementing one's too short bibliography with (unpublished) letters of denunciation, as a means of climbing the academic ladder are certainly characteristic not only for the Israeli nouveaux riches, but everywhere in "overstaffed institutions where people are furiously defending their right to their ignorance" (N. Mandelstam: Hope Against Hope)'.

In dedicating this book to my former students, some of whom have also chosen to explore the field of prejudices, I wish them success in their scientific endeavour and express the sincere hope that they will encounter less dishonesty than I did. However, should they at any time in the future have to choose between sycophantic conformism for the sake of their career and independence of thinking and freedom of expression, even if they have to pay a price for it, I hope they will choose the second way!

Tel Aviv, Summer 1972   G. R. T.

Editor's introduction

Israel is at war. In the course of its existence, the nation-state of Israel has been continually involved in serious hostilities, diplomatic as well as military - the latter including three major wars. Geographically almost encircled by its hostile neighbours, Israel has repeatedly sought to find a political squaring of the circle: being a peninsula of a rather remote political mainland together with being an island of autonomous military strength, and the reverse.

The very circumstances in which the process of nation-building of Israel took place inevitably inflicted a serious impact on the shaping of the Israeli cultural identity. Ideologically, the Israeli society had a choice of identifying with the norms and values of its political allies, or a rather rigid and militant adherence to (a part of) the 'cultural heritage' of its past. In fact, both types of identification played an important role in the evolution of the Israeli politico-ideological identity.

From a strictly logical point of view, many inconsistencies, stemming from these different frames of references, could be discerned. However, from a socio-psychological point of view, such a 'logical' would be rather futile and irrelevant for two reasons. First, owing to its position of relative isolation, the Israeli society adopted both courses primarily as rather intermingled elements within the context of a strong need for ideological consensus. Secondly, it should be stressed that on their part, both courses stimulated the relative isolation of the Israeli society, its political, religious and ethnic minority groupings and/or important sectors of the world community at large. For these reasons, any relevant research in this field has to deal, in one way or another, with these two aspects: the mutually reinforcing processes of cultural and political isolation, or in other words, Ghettoism.

Israel had to be a warfare state, characterized by a relatively high degree of military, political and ideological mobilization. Under such circumstances, any scientist who dares to throw his scientific doubts on the reliability of the dominant tenets of his society, risks his scientific career.

True, in this ideological sense, Israel does not offer the most striking example of a warfare state. Intellectual creativity and political idealism have been among the driving forces which promoted the creation of the state of Israel, and these forces have always played an important role in favour of an intellectuel climate of world-mindedness, of open-mindedness. On the other hand, theological dogmatism and nationalism - in its political manifestations of isolationism as well as annexionism - are also present among Israel's spiritual origins; and in the course of its existence as a warfare state these very forms of closed-mindedness had all the opportunities to become a dominant trait in the Israeli cultural Identity.

As a result, to some extent a process of insipidity occurred - as in any warfare state. In particular, those intellectuals who try to formulate criticism on the basic assumptions of daily life, expose themselves to serious negative sanctions. At best, they will politically be treated as gadflies, as a nuisance, at worst they will be condemned as traitors. If they continue, they will gradually become involved in a process of radicalism and of isolation. Intellectual criticism stimulates negative sanctions, and these sanctions in turn may lead to a much more firm and fundamental criticism which isolates the critic from his fellow-scientists and restrains them from positive action. A process of insipidity takes place: criticism loses its functions, the critic feels the stigma of being a 'non-integrated person' - regardless of the scientific merits and the validity of his criticism. Such was the situation that befell the author of this book.

Georges R. Tamarin was born in 1920. He grew up in Subotica, Yugoslavia. He studied psychology at the University of Zagreb, before and after the second world war. After having received his doctorate, he went to Israel. From 1949 until 1969 he worked as a psychologist in several hospitals in Israel and in France, and as a lecturer at the University of Tel Aviv. He is the author of more than sixty studies, many of them published in Croatian, English, French or German. This, as well as his many visits to scientific institutions all over the world might be indicative of Tamarin's cosmopolitan outlook - an outlook which gradually came into conflict with the predominant values of his social environment. Until about the middle of the sixties, most of his work (including some important theoretical and methodological investigations) consisted of studies in the field of psychopathology (studies on problems of disturbed identity, clinical casuistics and diagnostics). During the sixties, Tamarin found himself more and more confronted with symptoms of ghettoism. As any social scientist should do, he became interested in the origins, functions and dysfunctions of this politico-ideological phenomenon. As a psychotherapist, he had to stress the relevance of childhood experience and, consequently, he had to attack the educational system and its political and religious authorities. This was the beginning of the process of isolation I have already mentioned: in 1969 Georges Tamarin had to leave his chair at the University. A committee acknowledging Tamarin's very high scientific qualities, recommended by a 3:2 majority that he should be dismissed because of 'non-integration', which the Senate of the University endorsed. In the same year he founded a new institute, the institute of socio-psychological research, its name indicating his shift in interests.

When selecting the texts which compromise this book, the editor had taken into account several factors. First, this book should contain a number of studies on fundamental political and ideological problems within the Israeli social system, thus neglecting a lot of other work by the author. Secondly, this anthology should give some impression of the fields to which the author has dedicated his scientific life: theoretical explorations, empirical research, methodology, scientific criticism. The reader will find examples of all of these in this book. Thirdly, in some cases (Chs. 2, 3, 7) it was necessary to shorten the original versions of the various chapters considerably; in some other cases he had to confine himself to exclude some minor details. In all cases, however, the editor has sought to safeguard Tamarin's basic ideas.

Most of the studies collected here have been written and published in some form or another in the course of the last decade. Together, they should function as proof of intelligent mastership and scientific integrity.

Johan Niezing, Brussels, 1972,
Free University (VUB),
Polemological Centre

1. The Israeli dilemma: ghetto state or free society?*

I think the greatest peril in Israel is that of provincialism. Provincialism is a concept both of time and of space. A nation can be provincial by living only in the present; it can also become provincial, especially if it is a small people, by living exclusively within the limits of its geography.

A. Eban, 'Second Dialogue in Israel'

---

* B. Lessin lecture, Tel Aviv, 1965. From: 'Forms and Foundations of Israeli Theocracy', Shikpul Press, Tel Aviv 1968.

I certainly do not need to explain that the title of this book is a paraphrase of G. Myrdal's classic opus, 'An American Dilemma'.

In his well-known book, Myrdal emphasizes the crucial contradiction which is characteristic of the conflict of values and social practice, determined, on the one hand, by the democratic commandment of the 'American creed', and, on the other, by forces of egoism, group-prestige, prejudice and exploitation.

A contradiction, though dissimilar in form but analogous in spirit, also characterizes Israel's social and spiritual reality: the opposition between the 'Israeli creed' - the ideal of a democratic, egalitarian, progressive and enlightened society (presented by the official propaganda as an already accomplished, living reality) - and theocratic - racist laws, a chauvinistic atmosphere, parochial culture and the often totalitarian measures of the authorities.

This conflict is reflected in the antagonism between the tendencies orientated towards a physical and spiritual ghetto and those striving for a free and open society. This contradiction, as well as the dilemma as stated above, namely - whether the direction of development of the country progresses towards a harmonious integration in contemporary civilization, or towards enclosement, - is *the* Israeli problem. The solution of this problem will determine not only the socio-cultural physiognomy of the State, but, in my personal opinion, its political future as well.

Unfortunately, it is difficult to deny that simultaneously with brilliant achievements in the fields of soil reclamation, health, technology and partially also in the absorption of mass-immigration, enabling Israel to become a guide in those domains to underdeveloped countries and new nations, a constant aggressive strengthening of the forces of the ghetto, of religious obscurantism and nationalism is to be witnessed.

Among the most negative and alarming features of the actual development is the almost total paralysis of those forces whose *natural* role it is to tear down obsolete fences and traditional barriers - the rising generation. Because of an almost total lack of contact with the youth of other countries and as a result of the educational system, classes leave school, year after year, crippled in their general education and handicapped in their preparedness for higher studies as well as in their general outlook. Years will pass (and crises will follow) before they are able to overcome their parochial, intolerant and ethnocentric conceptions.

It is almost unnecessary to mention that one of the most sinister aspects of *any* ghetto is that one may not even feel its abnormality nor conceive that the world on the other side of the sacred walls is not necessarily one of hatred, impurity and abject customs; it is regarded as a sign of healthy patriotism not to reveal any interest in it.

So much has been written about the fact that we live in a period of electronic brains, atomic revolution, the conquest of space and the formation of supra-national economic and political units, when the fiction of national sovereignty becomes rhetorics, devoid of real content that it seems a commonplace to repeat it. And equally, there is no field in science, economy, sociology and ideology, where the urgent necessity is not felt to rethink the basic notions, as the axioms of yesterday become outdated, no less outdated than the horsedrawn carriage in the days of the steamengine, if one can draw any comparisons at all from the past which can serve, even partially, as an adequate analogy for the technological-social *mutation* of our times.

In this world of diminishing scientific and political frontiers, when *any* thinking on a national scale means an anachronistic and *ghettoic* vision of reality, even where physical and mental frontiers of the nation-state are much larger, more open, democratic and contemporary than those of Israel - one of the most significant developments in the social field is the acquaintance of a considerable number of the youth of various countries with foreign lands. Anyone who has met - in the youth hostels of Amsterdam, Rome or London - 16-18 year old boys and girls from Denmark, France, the USA and other countries, high-school students and young workers, speaking naturally about their forthcoming trip to Yugoslavia and Greece, exchanging impressions about the museums of Paris (where they were last year), or the routes in the Netherlands, or the social insurance of their respective countries, could hardly remain unimpressed by the broad scope of their horizons and the richness of their experiences. He will feel optimistic that these experiences will have an immunizing effect against the viruses of chauvinism, and that no distortions in the textbooks of national history, or demagogy of politicians, or drill in the army-camps will persuade them to believe the contrary to what they have witnessed with their own eyes.

Contrary to this, the mental horizons of Israeli youth of comparable age reveal an alarming picture: here, the great adventure is an excursion to Massada; the Gjernak (1208 m.) is synonymous with almost unattainable heights, and reading a simple sentence in a foreign language often requires very great effort. Mediocre movies and rare contact with foreigners are surely a feeble counter-balance to the influence of conservative teachers.

In Israel, the citizen has to pay an exorbitant foreign travel tax, in violation of his civil rights and against the international Convention to which the State subscribed, to be able to take a trip abroad. Even the authorities admit that the aim of this tax is not so much fiscal gain as 'to prevent Israelis from wandering around the world'. The Ministry of Education, as a faithful guardian of the spirit of the ghetto, also conceives its duty as fighting against the 'gluttony' of foreign travel. Different governmental bodies employ with various methods of chicanery and bureaucratic obstruction against the 'snob' who wants to see other countries, and against the unpatriotic attitudes of the generation which abandoned the pioneering ideals of single-minded devotion to the building of the country.

The regime's reluctance towards the citizen's contact with the world can be explained only by ghetto-orientated attitudes striving to build a closed society and to prevent acquaintance with present-day reality, unless it is through the channels of a conservative education and information derived from local sources. It also expresses the fear of the regime that the axiomatic values and deeply ingrained beliefs of the population may be shaken. The citizen may doubt that the prevention of mixed marriages is really compatible with democracy or that workers' representation necessarily means that almighty trade union bosses should, practically, be agents of the Treasury or of cooperative capitalistic enterprises.

The fruits of such education are inevitably a tendency to xenophobia, intolerance and prejudice, the manifestations of which will be the theme of this book.

One can often hear the argument - even from those who admit the narrow-minded and chauvinistic aspects of many phenomena of Israeli everyday life - that such indoctrination is necessary: a) in order to fight assimilation; b) because of the actual military situation of the country. To the question of assimilation I will return later. As to the second point, and without accepting the proposed justification, it is clear that any discussion of the ghettoic aspects of Israel must proceed from the fact that due to the 'no war, no peace' situation, Israel *is* a geo-political ghetto, whose only means of communication with the world is by sea (very expensive) and by air (even more expensive). This objective situation of an 'encircled fortress' determines many manifestations in the geo-physical ghetto in their primary and/or secondary aspects. Various psychological and social phenomena of prejudice and discrimination are also linked to this fundamental fact. Therefore, despite all the extreme differences of size, ideology, goals and the conduct of the authorities, there are some striking similarities between the Israeli encircled fortress and the Soviet ghetto before World War II, when that state, too, was a fortress besieged by enemies trying to annihilate it.

In both cases, in a closed society encircled by enemies and in a state of constant alertness, the ensuing phenomena are: a morbid sensitivity towards criticism, suspicion towards strangers, chauvinistic atmosphere, ideological intolerance, and a marked discrepancy between the letter of the law and its actual application by the authorities. In a closed society, the information received by the citizen is selective due to implicit and overt censorship and also due to a limited knowledge of foreign languages. Also, because of the warlike situation, limitations of civil rights are natural, and one can never know (except post factum from a historical perspective) which measures were really necessary for security reasons and which served the egoistic goals of the regime.

It is also evident that in such a situation, especially, when it becomes *chronic,* the citizens tend to lose their sensitivity for their rights and become accustomed to the infringement of their freedom. They will regard undemocratic steps of the authorities as a natural course of events and, especially if they have no opportunities for comparison or if chauvinism distorts their vision and dims their critical senses, they will soon become indifferent to denials of their civil rights.

It is difficult to decide whether the Israeli leadership gradually deteriorated as a result of becoming accustomed to the conditions of a ghetto, or whether this state of affairs suited its (perhaps latent) intentions. I can recall a conversation I had in 1951 with one of our prominent political leaders, who, when I expressed shock at the role of archaic taboos in public life and remarked that nowhere else in the world would it be conceivable to stop a state-owned railway from functioning on the Sabbath - he answered with a smile: 'What do you want? All this is temporary. In a few months, there will be peace and no religious fanatic will demand that the Beirut-Cairo train shouldn't cross Israel on the Sabbath.'

But the years have passed, peace is as far away as ever, the laws of the ghetto become worse from year to year... and the public is growing apathetic towards them.

I have no opportunity to assess the economic harm inflicted on Israel by the Arab boycott, but I have no doubt that the moral harm of the ghettoic encirclement is disastrous by its influence on the mentality of the population, although I also have no doubt that official circles will be shocked and infuriated by this statement.

An additional common explanation offered for prejudiced and discriminatory phenomena, at least regarding the laws governing marriage and other forms of religious coercion, is the necessity to form coalition governments and to make concessions to the religious governing partner.

This explanation is not only superficial, disguising more than it reveals, but it evades the necessary sociological analysis.

First of all, the 'coalition hypothesis' does not explain the process of the moral erosion of public and political life nor the deadly paralysis of individual consciences, when party or coalition discipline becomes the supreme ethical commandment. A typical example is the case of that Member of the Knesset who sharply criticized a proposed law, stating that 'We are deteriorating to the Middle Ages' - and yet voted for it without hesitation. Typical, too, is the by now axiomatic readiness of socialist ministers to pay for their coalition transactions by supporting racial-religious segregatory and similar laws.

Secondly, the coalition hypothesis throws no light on those circumstances which are the conditio sine qua non of such immoral coalition dealings - that is, the absence of a Constitution which would explicitly declare the basic rights of the citizen and thus restrict the unscrupulous trade with those rights. And, of course, no religious minority could prevent the legislation of a democratic Constitution, unless the machinery of the ruling secularist parties also wholeheartedly opposed such legislation.

Finally, in no way does this 'coalition hypothesis' explain why, at a given moment, when, following a general public uproar, the religious ministers themselves proposed the separation of the State from the Synagogue. The socialists, instead of joyously consenting, rejected this proposal in perplexity.

All these facts point to the conclusion expressed by Professor Bar-Hillel, that it is not always correct to speak about the exploitation of the State by the religious factions, but, on the contrary, the secularist regime exploits religion too, in order to achieve its own nationalistic goals: 'Those same authorities who do not openly dare to pass a law forbidding mixed marriages, let the Chief Rabbinate do the dirty work.'

In order to understand the ways and acts of the regime it is essential to take into consideration both certain ideological trends of Judaic history and the socio-psychological profile of the ruling class.

As to the question of historical tradition - we cannot overlook the fact that from ancient times, xenophobic intolerance has been one of the dominating trends in the social and spiritual realm of Judaism. Or, more exactly, from archaic times until the present day, two polar forces have been evident: the tendency towards enclosement from the world, and that of openness - the ghetto as opposed to universalism; narrow-minded nationalism and fanatic religiosity as opposed to cosmopolitan liberalism.

Illustrative of the liberal trend are some of the prophets; Hillel the Ancient, Jesus (without raising here the question of the historical or mythological nature of these figures); those who enacted the commandment, 'Thou shalt love the stranger'; the thinkers of the Alexandrian school, the early Caraites; Spinoza; Mendelssohn; Lamsdale; Buber; Einstein; Trotzky and the Jewish intelligentsia of the 19th and 20th centuries, which played a leading role in the struggle for national and social equality.

Illustrative of the second trend are: again, some of the prophets; the tribal taboo against dining or intermarrying with non-Jews; Shamai; Ezra; those rabbis who cursed anyone 'who raises pigs and who teaches his son Greek science'; the author of the commandment, 'The best of the Gentiles thou shalt kill'; those who burned Maimonides' books; those who anathematized Spinoza; the opponents of emancipation; and today, in Israel, the proponents of segregation in the style of the religious fanatics and the intolerant Zionist exclusiveness of Ben-Gurion. [1]

During the whole tragic history of the Jewish people, in different social and cultural conditions, one can witness the struggle between the spirit of the ghetto and that of freedom and universalism. Yet, sometimes (and also in the last recent decades) the fanatical mentality of the closed society passes into the heritage of those who fight against it. It manifests itself in their impulses and modes of thinking, sometimes as preconscious xenophobic reflexes and sometimes as an ideological design for a basically closed society.

The spirit of intolerance and segregation has a long tradition, characterizing, as stated above, some of the ideologists of the national renaissance, including those who define themselves as socialists. It is revealing, from this point of view, that in the interpretation of ancient Jewish history, the representatives of ultra-Orthodox Judaism, as well as the theoreticians of Zionism, describe in an unequivocally one-sided and negative light, sometimes as traitors, the representatives of trends open to the world such as Hellenists and other 'assimilationists'. The preference for enclosement and the affirmation of theocracy on the part of the first group is quite self-evident (in the past as well as today). However, the fact that the second group considers natural assimilation in an open and unsegregated society - where the relation of man to man is that of *free individuals,* for whom ethnic or religious origins create no barriers - as a greater evil than a national-religious ghetto (which will

---

1. Cf. 'Tolerance and Intolerance in Jewish Spiritual Heritage' (Ch. V).

preserve Jewish particularism) testifies to deep atavistic reflexes, characteristic also of most 'modern' nationalistic activists.

The ghetto, as a closed and immobile social structure in its physical and spiritual aspects, and its specific mentality was the natural structure of medieval society, progressively disintegrating in the world of industrialization, rationalism and political democracy. The last two hundred years have seen a period of the natural and irreversible dissolution of the ghetto. During this period, all the trends in Judaism: assimilation, secular and religious Zionism, the Bund, Communism, etc., have been searching for new ways in an *open w*orld in which the ghettos have become restricted - except in the Jewish *townlets* of Eastern Europe - to a few streets in Paris, Antwerp, New York, London, Bagdad, Tunis, and other places.

The disappearance of the closed and conservative ghetto may be inevitable. This is not only because of the fact that an ever increasing number of the inhabitants becomes free from its archaic taboo fears when the Enlightenment penetrates its walls and annihilates antiquated superstitions and customs, and not only because the younger generation, in ever growing numbers, leaves the physical and spiritual prison - but, first of all, because the ghettoic structure is *not viable*. The ghetto may have an original although undifferentiated culture (as all isolated societies, e.g., chassidic mysticism) but no civilization, civilization of electric power stations, mobile manpower, international systems of communication and scientific technology... as characteristic of industrial nations of the 20th century.

This is the principal reason for the irreversible and *natural* (that is, not caused by any anti-semitic aggressor) disappearance of the ghetto. In the last two hundred years, the ghetto has been in a state of constant *defensiveness,* even in the most technologically and culturally backward areas. It was also in a state of defensiveness in Palestine in the twenties and thirties (when these same rulers who today pass theocratic laws were fighting secularists). But today one can witness, for the first time, in the State of Israel, a *ruthlessly aggressive offensive* of the ghetto, with the aim of conquering the free society and impressing its imprint upon it. It either openly advocates coercion (Army Chief Rabbi Goren: 'The Torah prescribes coercion') or by transparent sophisms, it tries to prove, as Rabbi Kahane did, that racism is not racism, coercion is not coercion and discrimination is not discrimination (since the blow is equally distributed to both partners whom the segregratory laws have forbidden to marry). However, there *is* a truthful and undisguised statement in his article - that there is no justification in being angry with Orthodox Jewry for the apartheid laws, since these laws were passed by the *secular majority parties;* if there is someone to be reproached, then it is this same socialist majority which agreed to support and pass them.

At this point we must deal with the second aspect mentioned earlier: *the morphology of the ruling class of the state,* the character of the *elite* predominantly belonging to socialist parties, whose political-moral cynicism, partially, explains the unscrupulous trade in the civil rights of the citizen.

Israeli reality and the reactions of its leaders cannot be understood without taking into consideration the fact that they, almost without exception, grew up in those East European townlets which were the last de facto ghettos at the end of the 19th century, when the Jews, not only from democratic countries, but partly also from the *cities* of those same East European states had already lived for more than one generation in open and relatively enlightened societies.

Childhood in those townlets - learning in the *cheder* (from age 3-4), tales of their parents about pogroms and a constant feeling of persecution, inevitably shaped their personalities and modes of thinking - from the exclusive identification of Jewish tradition (the *yiddishkeit)* with the way of life of ultra-conservative and dogmatic Orthodoxy (which they despised in their pioneering years, but today, especially after their parents perished in the holocaust, embrace again and re-establish the suppressed sentimental ties) to deep subconscious xenophobic mechanisms.

In stressing the formative influence of life during childhood in those primitive townlets, I naturally do not have the intention of implying (even if that influence is very deep indeed) that this intolerance is a kind of inevitable 'constitutional-social' defect. Thousands of Jews originating from these same townlets later became, in various parts of Europe and America, pioneers in the struggle against any form of discrimination and for the full establishment of human rights, liberty and justice.

But - in those countries there existed a *tradition of the rights of the individual,* at least as an ideal, and the thinking concerning social progress unfolded in categories of the naturalness of achieving or safeguarding those basic rights. No such tradition existed either in the autocratic countries of East Europe, in Ottoman or Mandatory Palestine. This lack of a liberal and secular tradition seems to be (even if we disregard the before-mentioned historical trend of intolerance) the reason that the former inhabitants of those townlets have a sociological disposition towards dogmatism, not only as representatives of the religious orthodoxy, but also as protagonists of nationalism or socialist revolutionaries.

The importance of the tradition of the closed societies cannot be overestimated. The observation of Koestler pointing to the difference in approach between Jabotinsky and most other Zionist leaders should be mentioned here. Jabotinsky (who certainly cannot be accused of lack of national consciousness), who grew up in a big *city*, for instance, advocated Hebrew writing with *Latin characters,* so that it should be a medium of contact and not of separation in communication with other cultures, when speaking about the ruling class.

In order to be objective, one has to differentiate between at least two strata. One consists of the old, naive and mostly idealistic leaders, often members of kibbutzim, morally irreproachable, who still think in outdated categories which even forty years ago would have been considered socialistic if one identifies agrarian romanticism with socialism (Cf. Ch. 4: 'The Israeli Authoritarian Personality'). And, a second stratum: the nouveau riche, primitive, economic-political bureaucracy (far from being morally irreproachable) which holds key positions in various machineries of the State, the Jewish Agency, the Histadrut, the cooperative enterprises, etc. - in its greater part a parasitic class and the watch-dog of its own vested interests. By the very essence of its social character, it is an antiliberal and anti-intellectual factor, opposed to progress and imbued with totalitarian tendencies. Its conservatism is 'constitutional' since the first progressive change would be its liquidation and replacement by competent experts. Its lack of education, as well as its class-interests, make this stratum the protagonists of an antidemocratic regime and opponents of the opening of the closed society whose rulers they are. But as mentioned before, the differentiation between these two types within the ruling class has a predominantly subjective significance, more of intention and valuation than of action.

From an objective and public point of view, there is absolutely no difference if a capitalistic enterprise, being a politico-economic pressure group, obtains a monopoly over transportation for its own enrichment and the exploitation of the public (including practically, the right to pollute the air which the public breathes) whether this privilege is conferred by a corrupt bureaucrat or a highly virtuous old labor leader who, fascinated by the magic word, *cooperative,* is unable to see its capitalistic character and antisocial misuses. Or, if he, in the role of a courageous 'socialist' Don Quixote, fights against the 'satanic' purposes of private initiative and forbids chartered flights - with the inevitable result that tourists from the Scandinavian states (who have different concepts about civil rights and socialism) instead of coming to Israel, fly to Egypt, and foreign students cancel their visits, thus strengthening the ghettoic isolation of our youth. The *reactionary* character of these acts is the same as that of the *Neturei Karta* who segregate their children in suffocating old quarters, fearing 'contamination' by contact with the infidels.

The conclusion imposes itself: these ideologists *must* be - consciously or unconsciously - interested in the perpetuation of the ghetto, even by coercive measures.

My second qualification, namely, that the representatives of the spirit of the ghetto are by no means only the religious fanatics, may be, by now, somewhat superfluous.

True, it was Rabbi Levin who affirmed in the Knesset that there is no need for any other kind of education except that of the sacred writings, and Rabbi Porush who used the argument that his daughter had never seen a *Goy* to attract Western immigrants! But it was a member of Mapai who, during a Zionist Congress, proposed the expulsion of non-Jewish spouses. And members of various secular parties voted in the Knesset for the outlawing of pig-breeding.

I was told more than once by members of the left wing Hashomer Hazair kibbutzim, that while working in the dining room, they were asked by some of their comrades to warn them when pork was to be served, since the thought that they might swallow such meat, made them vomit. This almost organic fright (which is contrary to their conscious attitudes and readiness to eat, without hesitation, other non-kosher foods) reminds one again of the medieval demonologic reactions of terror during encounters with the *Impure*. It testifies to preconscious atavisms which are simply incomprehensible to someone - whether or not he is religious - who has grown up in an open society and for whom the tenets of religion are no longer identical with terrifying taboos, and for whom the image of a person of another religion or nationality is not determined by irrational feelings of repulsion, breaking through all the layers of his enlightened conceptions [2]. And for him whose childhood was not spent in the same suffocating quarters (inhabited by supersti-

---

2. It is quite unnecessary to mention that similar, nearly organic, unconscious representations concerning the diabolic character of Jews exist in many Christians, even today. It is enough to cite Sartre (Réflexions sur la question juive) who mentions someone who became impotent the moment he discovered that his mistress was a Jewess, and also many passages from Trachtenberg, 'The Devil and the Jew'.

tions and horrifying collective memories, under the despotic rule of autocratic rabbis, in an atmosphere where democratic dialogue and freedom of creation are totally unknown), it will be difficult to grasp that Shalom Asch was an object of fierce attacks in the trade union paper, 'Davar', and boycotted by large segments of the public, simply because he dared write novels about figures in the New Testament; that an Israeli socialist minister could not mobilize enough strength during his visit to the USA, to enter a reform synagogue; that the equally socialist President of the Republic, Ben Zvi, refused to participate in the dedication of the Biblical Archeological School in Jerusalem, since there was a reform synagogue in its grounds; that in Israeli schools the sign for plus is written differently than it is in the rest of the world ($\pm$) - so as not to make the sign of the cross; etc. etc.

Concerning the dogmatism of closed minds, I repeat, there may only be a difference of *content,* but not necessarily of *structure,* between the duty to accept without criticism the truth of 'collective ideology' and that of the Talmud, and as to the xenophobic reactions, there need not be any qualitative difference between the attitude of suspicion towards the 'corrupt' and tempting world outside the kibbutz or outside the Sabbath - belt of Bnei-Brak.

It was necessary, in order to understand specific Israeli reality, to emphasize the various elements which, consciously or unconsciously, for different reasons - from safeguarding the purity of the chosen people to safeguarding the values of an outdated socialist-national utopia - are adherents of a closed and isolated society, and afraid (consciously or not) of freedom and progress.

This adherence is true of the inhabitant of Mea Shearim, who is afraid his daughter might be 'contaminated' by contact with Zionists; of the reader of a *liberal* newspaper who in his letter to the editor insists on the *danger* of peace, since free contact with the neighbouring Arab states might increase mixed marriages; of the theoretician of the kibbutz movement who is perplexed by the confrontation with an affluent society, since under such conditions, the puritanical ideals of the kibbutz will lose their attractiveness; of the novelist, C. Hazaz (also a socialist and a close friend of Ben-Gurion) who is shocked by the physiognomy of contemporary American Jewry (so different from the traditional image) and proposes to send a 'peace corps' from Israel to save it... not to mention all those conservative elements whose economic and social interests are linked to the perpetuation of a ghetto-state.

All these factors present a serious obstacle to the radical modernization and development of Israel in the direction of an open society, and they also pose a serious threat to the admittance of the fact, as stated by A. Eban, that the greatest danger for Israel is provincialism. The intellectual and emotional inertia prevents *rethinking*, in the light of contemporary reality, of the basic problems of the State, of Judaism and of Mankind.

Without a revolutionary rethinking of the problems no progress is possible.

The representatives of separationist-Zionist nationalism (in *different* movements) and those of the religious Orthodoxy, curse the assimilationist 'traitors' with all the furor of traditional intolerance inherent in Jewish history - instead of analyzing this sociological phenomenon in a rational and objective manner. And even the leaders of left-wing Zionist parties justify their active or passive support of religious coercion and segregation laws by the necessity to *'strengthen* (the problematic) *Jewish identity'*.

Some remarks are indispensable in this context.

First of all, the question arises: if assimilation is a *natural* consequence of life in an open, free and unsegregated society and if the only defense against the threat of freedom is the erection of a (national or religious or racialist) ghetto - should the closed ghetto be *preferred* to assimilation? And, is a positive answer to this question compatible with the ideas of socialism, democracy, tolerance and respect for human rights?

Orthodox religious Jewry is sincere in its response: in the name of its absolute values it prefers the ghetto to assimilation. The secularist, supposedly democratic, nationalists do not dare answer openly in the same manner and they fly into distorted rationalizations to justify the policy of segregation.

Secondly, there are many cultural-spiritual currents in religious Judaism today which are far removed from the darkness of the ghetto and its intolerance, and to whom basic human rights (including the tenet that religion is a private matter) and religious tolerance are values no less cherished than the values of religion itself. Representatives of American Judaism stated repeatedly in an unambiguous manner their repulsion and abhorrence of religious coercion and terrorism in Israel.

Thirdly, it reveals a one-sided erroneous view, to speak about religion as a unifying and linking factor of Judaism. This may be *partly* true, and was true in the *past*, but it is no longer the case. It is an elementary thesis of modern sociology that religions which once had a functional and cohesive role may, under changed circumstances, become dysfunctional and disruptive.

And finally, it is quite ludicrous to hear the secular leadership speaking about *unity* (as conceived by the Orthodox) and thus justifying coercion - when the situation of the free thinking individual is that *of the prisoner chained to his jailer*. Such 'unity' is conceivable only in a frame of reference where ideas of freedom and free choice are totally absent.

When I lectured about the results of some of my research - violating many of our sacrosanct taboos - I sometimes encountered outbursts by a section of the public which reminded me of similar experiences with the ultra-nationalistic and clerical groups in my former European homeland. I have no intention of entering into a discussion with these 'critics'; the manifestations of which are only additional proof of my formulations concerning intolerance in Israel.

At this point I should like to clarify some aspects of the fact that I place great emphasis on the *negative* phenomena, presenting a subjective picture of Israel, instead of discussing the totality of light and shadow.

I certainly agree that phenomena should be studied and presented in their totality. But, I do not understand a balanced approach using the technique of 'counterpoints' in the style of the Soviet Union. Yes, the Soviets were the first to launch the Sputniks, *but* there is no freedom there; or, Yes, the USA is the leading industrial power, *but* there is anti-Negro segregation there; not to mention the remark of that 'critic' of Yevtushenko (a young officer) who 'eliminated' the gruesome tragic theme of Babi Yar: 'Why does he write about sad topics, and not about something cheerful, for example, on life in the Soviet Army?'

The above remark reveals a basic misunderstanding: I am not writing a topography of Israeli society, nor a psycho-sociological analysis of its different groups, *but about prejudice* in this society. Therefore, my theme, per definitionem, determines the predominance of the negative elements, just as one finds little sublime motive in a treatise about criminology, or as the symptoms of syphilis are a rather unpleasant sight, even if they appear on the body of the most courageous hero.

It is a controversial subject in social psychology whether prejudices should be considered 'normal' or 'pathological' social phenomena, but it is without doubt that they reveal the *worst side* of any individual, national (religious, etc.) group, and even culture. Israel is no exception in this respect.

This should be clear to all those who object to research on prejudice and publication of its results, motivated by fear that those data can be used and misused by enemy propaganda. It is the duty of any scientist worthy of the name to speak *frankly* about his investigations, without concealing facts or opinions.

Any book dealing with the sociology of Israel has to present all the aspects of its socio-dynamics, all the light and the shadow, and all the 'counterpoints'.

Such a treatise should objectively point out that many of the same teachers who today, as an ultra-conservative group, implant narrow-minded chauvinism in their pupils, risked their lives as heroes during World War II in order to rescue 'illegal' refugees persecuted by British warships, that many of these same bureaucrats, who are today's primitive nouveaux riches, were once sincere idealists, socialists and pioneers; that if today the Workers' Sick Fund is a reactionary organization, politically enslaving the workers and hampering the development of medical services, when founded - it was an enormous contribution to the labour movements and health services of the Middle East, and not only of Palestine, etc., etc.

And if it is objectively true that Israel is characterized by many anti-democratic and prejudiced features, it is equally true that it has also progressive and egalitarian traits, and *that so long as our planet is divided into anachronistic national states the existence of Israel has its absolute moral justification, particularly in view of the tragic past of the Jewish people and the still virulent anti-semitism in many countries, perhaps even more so than some contemporary estatistic formations.*

But this, again, is by no means a reason for a conspiracy of silence that would mask the negative phenomena, or that these phenomena should not be openly criticized and contested.

And since, as mentioned, a rather general paralysis of individual rights and freedom is spreading, and a distorted way of thinking and presenting facts tends to disguise prejudice and to present totalitarian denials of human rights as compatible with democracy and enlightenment - the unmasking of these trends is urgent, and should be done in unequivocal terms.

It is ridiculous to suggest freedom and democracy when even such leaders as Goldmann and Sharett, who criticize the anachronistic and anti-humanistic marriage and divorce laws, would be content with a little more liberal interpretation of the Halacha on the part of the Orthodox Rabbinate and with reforms concerning the laws forbidding marriage of a cohen and a divorcee and yet not acknowledge the absolute right of the individual to marry or divorce without interference from any religious authority. Or, if even A. Eban, one of the few who see the problems of the land not from a ghettoic perspective and who is only too well acquainted with the fundamentals of a democratic society, dares to state that: 'I have never known of any disaster occur through getting married in a religious ceremony, even if they don't happen to believe in religion'. What degree of perverted (or simply demagogic) thinking prevents one from seeing the truth, that there is no difference in forcing a secular Jew to marry by religious ritual, than to force an Orthodox Jew to act against the tenets of his belief. And that it is shameful that Israel failed to subscribe to the Convention on Freedom of Religion.

It is an expression of perverted thinking to speak about freedom and democracy if the reform projects are restricted to an arrangement for a somewhat better-aired prison and that the prisoner should have the right to several days leave. The basic democratic requirement is that the State should not be a theocratic prison governed by religious-racialist laws. If the designation 'prison' seems too strong, it should not be forgotten that the favoured expressions of the Orthodox groups are: the walls of the Sabbath; a crack in the wall separating Jews and Gentiles, etc. The fact that the walls of the ghetto-fortress are walls of a prison to freedom-loving men can surprise only those who never knew life outside a theocratic society.

There are no gradual improvements of prisons and ghettos; neither should immoral compromises, to avoid *Kulturkampf*, be presented as achievements. In the words of the great fighter for the rights of his people, J. Baldwin: 'A ghetto can be improved in one way only: out of existence'. It is of paramount importance that the Israeli public should grasp the simple fact: neither physical, economical, nor moral laws change when they reach the Israeli custom house. And there can be no one-way democracy - requiring tolerance and freedom for oneself, and at the same time, justifying the right to be intolerant and to persecute others.

And since a very dangerous *double-think* and *double-talk system* has become prevalent in Israeli public life (making it difficult to judge whether one deals with schizophrenia of political thought which believes its own words, or with cynical lies) those elementary facts have to be stated quite clearly. It is not enough to vote against racialism in South Africa and Rhodesia; one also has to abolish barriers of religious-national *apartheid* in Israel. No public can be fooled forever with double-talk: 'We will maintain the freedom of traffic movement by all means... and by adequate detours' (we succumb to the blackmail demands of the Orthodox), 'The discriminations against the community of Bnei Israel are now abolished' (the wording of the manifestly discriminatory rules has changed, but the racialist content has remained); 'Freedom of religion and conscience' (theocratic rule of the Orthodoxy); 'Prolongation of the working agreements' (instead, the tabooed truth: blocking of salaries, by consent of the bosses of the trade unions, executors of governmental policy); 'voluntary surrender to the decision of the rabbis' (brutal coercion of an unfortunate divorcee); 'The minorities are citizens with full equality of rights' (except that they are at the mercy of the Military Government); 'We support tolerance and unity and will prevent anything that may hurt the feelings of some of our members' (not to irritate the intolerant Orthodox, we will prevent Reformist worship), etc., etc.

The Israeli public has to understand several factors:
— The absolutely legitimate request that every Jew has the right to immigrate to Israel is valid only if he has the right to leave if he wants to, without any administrative hindrance, and without being called a traitor; and not in order to exchange the status of a captive of one state for that of another.
— The request that every Jew in Moscow who wants to eat matzot on Passover should be able to do so is valid only if every Jew in Jerusalem who wants to eat bread on Passover can also do the same.
— If a landlord in Paris or Boston refuses to lease a room to a Jew, it is no better if a landlord in Tel Aviv refuses to lease a room to an Arab.
— If it is an inhuman atrocity when Jewish children in Poland or Argentina are boycotted or persecuted by their peers because they are circumcised, it is by no means better if uncircumcised (Jewish or non-Jewish) children are boycotted and persecuted in Israel.
— It is true that the Bible is one of the greatest creations of human cultures. but it is equally true that it is full of inhuman motives and that, as Koestler (who surely cannot be accused of being an antisemite) states, all the bases of the Nuremberg Laws can be found in it, and that, therefore, children should not be bound to identify with its tenets and heroes.
— If the segregatory laws of the *Herrenrasse* were barbarous, the segregatory laws of the chosen people are equally barbarous.

Israeli politicians speak much about Israel's responsibility towards *World Jewry* (thus justifying many of its discriminatory laws), but they forget that Israel's first duty towards world Jewry should be putting an end to the situation as described by W. Maslow when protesting in the name of the World Jewish Congress against intolerance towards some Jewish groups, he almost immediately heard the reply: 'But in Israel, intolerance is even much worse'.

The ghettoic thinking distorts the vision of a very considerable number of Israel's politicians and even that of many of its intellectuals. It makes them captives of an outdated reality, values and modes of thinking which are, in the extreme, based on Biblical analogies, at best - embedded in nineteenth century nationalist categories.

All these are symptoms of a dangerous mental and political *immobilism*. The idea of *status quo* concerning religious matters became an almost magic and sanctified expression of the social realm. But, a generalized tendency of upholding an *immobile (istic)* status quo in other fields - except in military technology and partially in industry - is equally a significant feature of Israeli life.

These strivings towards conservative immobilism justify my contention that the solution of the Israeli dilemma, ossification as a ghetto state or progress in the direction of an open society, is dependent not only on its socio-cultural, but possibly its political future. This could also mean progress towards a peaceful settlement. The Israeli old-time ruling class can hardly adjust itself to present-day realities - they are 'monopolists' of visionarism concerning a very distant, almost messianic future, which is conceived in the categories of biblical notions and prophecies, but they have little imagination for conceiving the immediate future of our dramatic Atomic Age. I do not have the least intention of implying that they do not want peace, even though it can be assumed that for some of them, the no-war, no-peace situation has its tempting elements. For some, because it contributes to the cohesion of the nation and its readiness for sacrifice (this is exactly parallelled on the part of Arab leaders); for others, because open frontiers would mean increasing the 'danger' of mixed marriage. Peace evidently depends primarily on the Arab states, and it is an undisputable fact that chauvinism (incomparably more aggressive than in Israel) and often genocidal hatred prevail on the other side of the armistice demarcation lines and it is questionable when the tenet of destruction of Israel as a proof of 'true Arabism' will be abandoned.

What I want to say is that as long as the ghettoic reflexes of the Israeli elite and a sizable part of its population prevent the possibility of realising a desirable development, which is not necessarily in the category of closed national states with a homogeneous population, as long as the ghetto retains attractive features for national, religious or other reasons and as long as the development towards a free society causes conscious or unconscious perplexity - the strivings towards a closed society will prevent the necessary *revolutionary rethinking* of present-day problems. This hampers attainment on the road leading to an open society and it could also obstruct the path leading to peace.

2. Legal bases of prejudice and discrimination in Israeli society *

Everyone is entitled to all the rights and freedoms set forth in this Declaration without distinction of any kind such as race, colour, sex, language, religion, political or other opinion, national or social origin, birth or other status.

Declaration of Human Rights II/1

The liberty to follow one's religion and ritual is, of course, one of the fundamentals of Israel. Moreover, the State maintains religious services for all creeds, at the expense of the taxpayer. Only with us the shoe is on the other foot. It is not the religious people who claim freedom to worship God; so much is freely and willingly given to them. It is the non-observant and non-religious who want to be free to behave according to their wish.

G. Hausner (4)

---

* From: 'Forms and Foundations of Israeli Theocracy', Shikpul Press, Tel Aviv, 1968.
The author is indebtful to Dr. A. Rubinstein for reading this chapter and for his helpful remarks.

I. One of the first questions a study of prejudices in a given society poses concerns their legal sources. The reason is not only because it proves their *institutionalized* character and that the very fact of their legality indicates that the degree of intolerance (according to the accepted criteria of the Subcommittee for Human Rights of the United Nations (7)) in this society is among the highest in a specific segment of social life; but also because the fact of thus being legalized lends the discriminatory practices a special significance and influence on the public mind, different from that of purely social discrimination, without legal consecration, or even contrary to the written law.

True, written law is in itself neither a guarantee of liberal practices nor proof of anti-democratic practices. Social conventions may be (for better or for worse) stronger than the letter of the law; and especially if the law contradicts deeply-rooted mores, if it is outdated or otherwise senseless.

For instance, in France it is still illegal to sell contraceptives, yet one can buy them in every pharmacy, and the 'transgressor' will be neither punished nor considered by his environment as an immoral person. On the other hand, while in most states of the USA, there is no legal barrier to interracial (or in India, to inter-caste) marriage, one may become an outcast, or even the object of physical assault if one violates the existing *unwritten* segregatory laws. And the Soviet citizen who takes seriously the freedom of expression guaranteed by his constitution may easily find himself in prison. But on the whole, if racist or otherwise discriminatory practices are institutionalized and also approved by law, they will probably be more firmly anchored.

Discriminatory practices (in the widest sense of the word, encompassing all forms of intolerance) have a legal foundation in Israel in three (partially overlapping) fields: 1) denial of some basic human rights by segregatory and other laws; 2) violation of the freedom of conscience by religious coercion; and 3) discriminatory regulations concerning the Arab minority.

The fourth (and fifth) area of prejudiced ideas and behaviour - as enumerated in the Chapter I - has no legal basis whatsoever. On the contrary: the inter-community phenomena of prejudice among the various Jewish communities, especially the haughty attitude on the part of some Ashkenazis towards the 'non-Western' Jews, or prejudices of old timers against new immigrants [1] are wholly of a social nature, and in contradiction to the declared aims of the authorities.

1. We shall refrain here from dealing with the specific question of new immi-

II. Before exposing the *positive* laws on which religious coercion in the State is based, most of which simultaneously imply a denial of basic rights of the individual, and sometimes also have a racial-national-religious discriminating-segregatory character, the *absence* of a *constitution* which would define the State as a secular democratic one has to be stressed. Such a Constitution would remove the basis from a legislation which reminds one of the Middle Ages and turns Israel, at least partially, into a de facto theocracy. Furthermore, such a democratic Constitution would also end the state of affairs in which the secularist citizen is forced to finance religious services, such as building synagogues, ritual baths, yeshivoth, kashruth inspectors, clerks of Religious Councils, etc., whose services are not only superfluous, but, to make the irony of the fact more bitter, whose task and aim is to impose restrictions on his diet and his freedom of movement. By the same token, the very fact of the existence of a Ministry of Religious Affairs at the expense of the secular citizen is against the spirit and traditions of democracy, and - to make things worse - this Ministry is, with rare exceptions, held not by a neutral personality, but by representatives of a fundamentalist Jewish Orthodox party, whose avowed goal is to impose by all available means an Orthodox way of life on the Jewish population, and whose activities perhaps more often than not, border on illegal practices. The same is true for the Religious Councils whose composition, according to an agreement between Mapai and the National Religious Party, automatically grants the Orthodox representatives a majority, even if the population of a specific locality is totally non-religious - an agreement censured as immoral by the Supreme Court.

In this author's opinion, the most anti-democratic and reactionary law, since it legalizes religious-racial discriminatory practices and serves

grants. There are very few formal discriminatory measures concerning them (principally in obtaining passports). Practical discriminations are based much more on the fact that in many aspects of their absorption they depend not on the authorities of the State, but on the Jewish Agency. The officials of the latter allow themselves arbitrary steps towards the immigrants such as the officials of the State would never contemplate. Illustrative is the request to the police that they remove by force from the ships those immigrants who refuse to go to the places the Jewish Agency has allocated to them, a totally unlawful action. Or, discriminating against immigrants living in mixed marriage, by allocating them to bachelors' flats. One of the officials explained to me: 'The State could never do such a thing, but the Agency, which represents the Jewry of the world, is entitled to give from the contributions of Jews only to Jews, and not to non-Jews.' (I am sure that world Jewry in its overwhelming majority would be deeply shocked by this philosophy.)

as a foundation of the theocratic fabric of Israeli public life, is that of the 'Jurisdiction of Rabbinical Courts (Marriage and Divorce) 1953', a (modified) descendant of Mandatory legislation, establishing that issues of personal status in these matters will be based on religious-community laws [2].

Additional laws which constitute either direct (Orthodox) religious coercion or at least a de facto religious interference in the life of the individual and the public, either by their proper text or in their customary, discriminatory usage, are: 'The Work and Rest Hours Law, 1951', 'The Council of the Chief Rabbinate (Elections) Law, 1963', 'The Anatomy and Pathology Law, 1953', 'The Prohibition of Pig-Breeding Law, 1962', 'The Defense Service Law, 1949, 1959', 'The Legal Competence and Guardianship Law, 1962', 'The Kosher Food for Soldiers Ordinance, 1948', as well as some of the Standing Orders of the General Staff, and various Municipal by-laws (partly legal and partly illegal).

Denoting the law of personal status regulating marriage and divorce as the most reactionary, we had in mind its content, as well as its practical influences:

a. Creating a situation of apartheid by the prevention of mixed marriages between Jews and non-Jews, and also between Jews of some sects and communities, thereby flagrantly violating Paragraph 16 of the Declaration of Human Rights of the United Nations [3]. This law (which reminds at least many of the European immigrants of similar provisions in the infamous Nuremberg Laws, forbidding mixed marriages) from a socio-psychological point of view, is one of the principal sources of prejudice, influencing also the non-religious but chauvinistic section of the public in their rejecting attitude towards 'Goyim' (meaning here 'non-kosher' Jews and/or non-Jewish spouses and their offspring).

b. Creating a category of judges ('dayanim') who do not pledge to judge according to the laws of the State; at the same time, discriminating

---

2. According to this law, 'The issues of marriage and divorce of the Jews, citizens or residents of the State, will be under the exclusive jurisdiction of rabbinical courts'. We defined this law as the most dangerous, since it concerns the dominant majority of the country's population, and it is also the most intolerant, because Jewish religious law denies *any* possibility of mixed marriage.

3. Men and women of full age without any limitation due to race, nationality or religion have the right to marry and to found a family. They have equal rights as to marriage, during marriage and at its dissolution, Declaration of Human Rights XVI/1.

against women, who cannot be appointed 'dayanim'; and discriminating between two kinds of lawyers, those entitled to appear before the religious courts and those who are not so entitled. Also, discriminating between Orthodox rabbis entitled to perform marriage and divorce ceremonies, and those of the other branches of Judaism, who are prevented from either function.

c. Endorsing the principle of inequality of women (who cannot obtain divorce without the consent of the husband). The 'Law of Equality of Women', 1953 explicitly states its non-applicability to the laws of marriage and divorce. This inequality clearly contradicts Paragraph II/1 of the Declaration of Human Rights.

d. Causing uncertainty as to the validity of mixed (and other) marriages (and divorces) of couples who married or divorced according to civil law abroad (or even were married by a Reform Rabbi), thus violating the respective principles of International Private Law.

e. Endorsing the principle of inequality between Jews and non-Jews (the latter being invalidated as witnesses before the religious courts) and the inequality between 'kosher Jews' and 'bastards' [4], a term which no longer appears in the laws of any enlightened country, thereby contradicting the principle of equality of men and the above-mentioned paragraph on the Declaration of Human Rights.

f. Creating inequality concerning *positive arrangements* between persons belonging to a recognized religious denomination, on the one hand, and those who belong to unrecognized ones, and atheists, on the other (the latter having no positive arrangement at all which would enable them to marry and to divorce).

g. Violating the freedom of conscience by forcing non-religious persons to get married (and divorced) in an Orthodox religious ceremony and sometimes even to undergo religious conversion in order to be able to marry.

---

4. As to the different meaning of the term 'bastard' in Rabbinical Judaism from that in most countries, see J. Ben Menashe (3) and also his discussion of the fictitious 'danger' that 'civil marriage would lead to the creation of a generation of bastards'. This recurrent argument of the Orthodox activists is also refuted by Prof. J. Leibovitz, himself an Orthodox scientist, basing his arguments on Halachic law. (Cf. his 'Separation of Religion and State', in 'Beterem').

h. Denying the right of the Supreme Court of the State to rule concerning the validity of 'forbidden marriages' (i.e. forbidden by religious law).

i. Preventing the possibility of remarriage to some widows and forsaken wives and preventing a divorcee from marrying her beloved, if they were lovers during her marriage (which was the reason for the divorce!).

j. Creating legal and social absurdities due to conflicting laws, for example, the fact that the same person is a Moslem, because of his father (according to Islamic law) and a Jew, because of his mother (according to Jewish Halachic law) when both laws are equally valid. He therefore lacks a personal status and is unable to marry.

Speaking about the discriminations stemming from this law, Ben Menashe (3) enumerates:

'We have to pause for a moment on the issue of religious conversion. To all those who state that if a non-Jewish woman wants to marry a Jew, she has to convert, one has to answer that the matter violates the freedom of conscience of the rabbis, since it is known that a conversion to Judaism not out of conviction is objectionable, and 99 per cent of the conversions are not out of conviction, and the rabbis are right in refusing to convert, but that does not mean that the State has to stand by passively in the face of such a situation.

In the country there are people who married abroad according to rabbinical law, but divorced according to civil law, or they were married by rabbis who are not recognized by the rabbis who rule in the land, and according to the existing religious laws, their right to establish a lawful family life is denied.

According to the laws which exist in our country, the family situation of many couples is characterized by such absurdities that the mind boggles. A Jew and a Christian woman, or a Moslem and a Jewess are considered by Moslem or Christian law as married, and as bachelors by Jewish law, i.e., one of the partners is 'married' and the other is 'single'.

The principle of equality and non-discrimination is considered, similar to that of freedom of conscience, one of the sanctified values of a democratic regime. There are many discriminations in personal status. It may be that this is good and proper from the religious point of view; however, since this discrimination is binding for secularists and persons of religions other than the dominant one, things appear in another light. Due to the existing laws, citizens are discriminated against due to their community affiliation; citizens who do not belong to a recognized community are completely unable to marry; and citizens belonging to two different communities cannot marry each other. In Israel a Rabbinic Jew cannot marry a Caraite Jew; Israeli Catholic Christian is unable to marry Israeli Orthodox Christian; marriages of Protestants are illegal, and so on.

— Due to their origin, a non-Jewish woman, even if she converted, cannot marry a man whose origin is from a family named 'Cohen', 'Katz', 'Kaplan', 'Rapaport', and so on.

- Due to their name, a man whose name is 'Cohen', 'Katz', 'Kaplan', 'Rapaport', and so on, is not allowed to marry a divorcee, not even to remarry his own divorced wife - not even if they have children.
- In witnessing, a non-Jewish Israeli citizen is a priori invalidated from testifying before a rabbinical court in cases of marriage and divorce, even if his testimony is vital for the execution of justice.
- Between man and woman, the man can marry a second woman if his wife is declared to be insane, but the wife is always chained to the husband, even if he is declared insane and her fate is to be an 'aguna' until the end of her life.

This survey would not be complete without mentioning the issue of 'Bnei Israel'. From the point of view of the rabbis, there is here also an injury to their conscience. If a rabbi, bona fide, refuses to marry 'Bnei Israel', he should not be forced to do so against his conscience, not even for political reasons, as is done, but the State, again, should not be a neutral observer. Only civil marriage will solve the problem of Bnei Israel.'

A few cases will suffice to illustrate the absurd and inhuman situation. For instance, a case requesting the appointment of a guardian for a child born out of wedlock by a Moslem father and a Jewish mother came before the courts. The judges of the Supreme Court who finally gave in the last instance their verdict, refrained from deciding the child's national-religious status; in appointing the guardian they took into consideration (as to the personality of the guardian) solely the benefit of the child, completely disregarding religious arguments - but simultaneously leaving the child without personal status. In another similar case, where the parents *did* want to marry, the Ministry of Social Affairs (held by the Orthodox) obtained a decision from a magistrate, stating that the mother was unfit to raise her child and that he should be put into an institution. The unfortunate mother was forced to steal her child. The scandal which arose forced the authorities to renounce their plan, and the couple was married by civil marriage in Cyprus.

Typical of thousands of couples and their children is the case of the Akwitz family.

'It is enough to mention as an example, the case of the Akwitz family, which, in its time, caused a public uproar. This family came to Israel from Russia. The father was a Jew, the mother of Russian origin. They had two children. In their land of origin they were lawfully married. There, the father and his children were considered as Jews, and, therefore, they decided to come to the land of the Jews. The mother, similar to Ruth, the Moabite, in her time, said: 'Thy people are my people, where thou shalt go I shall go', and joined the immigrants. But here, a very unpleasant surprise awaited them. When the son grew up and the time came to enlist in the Army, he turned to the Registry of Residents to obtain an identity card. To the surprise of the whole family, he was identified as a Russian and a Christian.

The fact that his father was a Jew and he was an Israeli citizen by the Law of Return, did not help.

According to the law applying to personal status in Israel, it was as if the father had not married his wife at all, and as if his children were not his children, but only of their mother; and so it is that father and son belong to two different nations and two different religions. The shock felt by this family was intense, and they left Israel and returned to their country of origin. The Akwitz family is only one example.' (2)

The incoherent and intrinsic paradoxes of the existing situation are accentuated by the fact that in those same religious laws, one can also find a (though very questionable and complicated) remedy - that of the so-called 'private marriages'. This, apart from the more expensive possibility of travelling to nearby Cyprus, or marrying by mail (the so-called 'Mexican marriages', introduced by attorney J. Ben Menashe, one of the indefatigable fighters against religious coercion) is a further step to outwitting the barriers of Orthodox law and partially also the violation of freedom of conscience of free thinkers. Since the Halachic law does *not* require the presence of a rabbi, but only the pronouncement of a prescribed dictum in the presence of two Jewish witnesses, these marriages (even the forbidden ones, except for those which are a priori void) are considered as valid, the rabbinical courts being forced to recognize them, or at least to declare that the marital status of the couple is in doubt and that they, therefore, have to divorce if they want to (re)marry. Since the Supreme Court did not recognize the formula of the status of 'not married and not not married', the Registry of Residents was obliged despite the opposition of the Orthodox, to register them as married.

Although the Supreme Court voiced sharp criticism as to the arrangement of private marriages, pointing out the danger to public order inherent in them, and even that if a third party (eg., an attorney) arranges such a marriage, he is liable to criminal prosecution, the couple is free to do so; moreover, in commenting upon such a case, Justice Landau said:

'I do not see justification for indignation because of the behavior of the applicants, because of the trick they used in arranging the 'private' marriage ceremony, (a domain) where our State promises freedom of conscience to all its citizens. The applicants are not observers of (religious) commandments, and according to the laws of the State, they are free to behave so. They want to live a married life and to raise children, in a way that the social stigma of 'outside of wedlock' should not cling to them. They encounter an interdiction which is wholly religious-ritualistic, since it is based on the archaic notion of the superior status of the cohen in (the performance of) sacred tasks. To impose such a prohibition on a non-believer is difficult to reconcile with the freedom of conscience and freedom of action inherent in it (......)'.

Another absurdity, of legalized (?) although temporary bigamy results from the ancient custom of *halitza*, jealously maintained by the Orthodox of our Atomic Age - as exemplified by the following case.

A deaf-mute couple from Ashdod married before yesterday for only one day, and this, instead of halitza that the bridegroom was obliged to give his new wife, who is the widow of his deceased brother. The marriage of one day was especially approved by the Chief Rabbis, Rabbi Nissim and Rabbi Untermann, since the bridegroom is married to another woman and is the father of a 10-month old daughter. The following morning, the divorce ceremony was conducted at the Rehovot Rabbinate.

The marriage of the couple was approved as a solution to the problem regarding the halitza, because according to the Halacha they are unable to perform the ritual of halitza that requires their saying a few words.

After the marriage ritual in the presence of the two rabbis of the town of Ashdod, the couple was transferred (sic) to a hotel room leased by the Rabbinate in order to execute the commandment to multiply. In order to ascertain that the promised divorce would be granted, the rabbis ruled that the bridegroom had to pay IL. 500 alimony per month to his new wife as long as they were married. (Ha'aretz, 5.3.67).

The above-mentioned facts show quite clearly that apart from excepting the racist laws existing in South Africa (and in some southern states of the USA), the laws of Italy and four backward Catholic states inspired by the Catholic Church, in no enlightened state do similarly reactionary and anti-human laws govern the citizen's most intimate realm of life.

The just-noted situation is a remarkable feature of Israeli social and political development - it is the secular state which established a centralized authority of a rigid, uncompromising and reactionary Synagogue.

'For 2,000 years, the Jews have been a sect based upon voluntary adherence. The rabbis had no powers of coercion, except those occasionally granted to them by the non-Jewish State for fiscal or other reasons. In the last analysis only those who so desired obeyed the rabbinical writ. There were, of course, ecclesiastical sanctions, but a Jew who was prepared to brave them had already, to all intents and purposes, left the fold. (......)

There are, on the other hand, powerful institutional factors encouraging Orthodox militancy. As is well-known, a Jewish rabbi has no charismatic powers, such as are attached to Apostolic succession and the power of sacrament. He is merely a learned man employed in a certain job. Judaism has no doctrine or even tradition of a centralized ecclesiastical organization, because, for one thing, the Jews are a people of priests. There has been no Supreme ecclesiastical authority in Jewry since the Sanhedrin ceased to exist. No official function, but the authority of superior learning and piety gives the ultimate sanction. It has happened very often that the law was laid down by a saintly learned layman in a God-forsaken townlet in Lithuania, who held no rabbinical office, but whose decisions no chief rabbi of a great country would presume to question. The

Chief Rabbinate is altogether an institution unknown in Jewish law, and in those countries where it exists, it came into being as a matter of administrative convenience. Not sovereign power, but moral authority was obeyed in Judaism. Various people (and communities) would bow to different authorities. In Israel today, the Rabbinate is rapidly developing into a firmly institutionalized Church imposing an exacting discipline on its members and facing the general body of laymen as a distinct power. This is not a religious development, but, ironically enough, the outcome of the emergence of the State. The latter has given birth and legitimacy to an established church.' (5)

The 'Council of the Chief Rabbinate (Elections) Law, 1963' which was also passed by the secular State, tacitly proceeds from the assumption that Judaism is *uniform* and *homogeneous,* and exclusively of the *orthodox* type (i.e., based on Halachic law) and whose rabbis are elected to the post of Chief Rabbi also (ruling over the non-Orthodox religious and non-religious population). It thus grossly discriminates against the other currents, imposing, de facto, the Orthodox current as the only valid Judaism. In the light of such a situation (and even disregarding the many non-legal discriminations; see the following chapters) it is small wonder that the statement of the Israeli Minister of Religious Affairs, made in the USA, that 'In Israel, there exists unlimited religious freedom' provoked the response of American Conservative and Reform rabbis that such freedom exists only in the unlimited and unrestricted phantasy of the Minister.

The same monopoly is mirrored also in the composition of the Council supervising the Religious Trend of the Public Schools (established in accordance with the law of compulsory education) - religious is equated with Orthodox and the inspectors and Council members (having the right to dismiss any teacher and to remove any pupil 'on religious grounds') are activists of the NRP.

The 'Defense Service Law, 1949, 1959', or, more exactly, its paragraphs which grant an exemption from service on grounds of *religion or conscience,* speaks about reasons of religion *or* conscience, but exemption is given only to those who declare themselves to be religious. A representative of the Orthodox political parties is often present at the committees deciding on such cases. However, this does not prevent many girls learning the 'right answers' and being exempt, while others, instead of continuing their studies or learning a profession, have to spend two years in an Army camp. Their practical usefulness for defense purposes is, according to many experts, questionable, but the Army service of girls is necessary for 'educational' reasons, according to the sanctified formula of: *'Zahal* - the school of the nation'.

The same moral (and sometimes not only moral) corruption also often works regarding the exemption of youngsters from the Druze villages, where the attainment of a certificate proving the religiousness of the applicant can depend very much on one's personal relationship with the local sheikh.

In addition to the above-mentioned ordinance forcing *all* soldiers to eat only kosher, there are many ordinances in the Standing Orders of the General Staff which resemble religious coercion. It is enough to mention the prohibition against the use of radios in army camps on Sabbath (while at the same time, the *Zahal*-waves transmit... apparently, only to civilians!); forcing of non-religious soldiers to participate in the religious 'days of awakening' before the high holidays; no provision of fresh food on Sabbath; and in some camps, due to the overzealousness of unit commanders (or more exactly, the sergeants of religion), obliging soldiers to carry heavy cauldrons to distant places in order not to transport them by trucks from the central kitchen; the prohibition against accepting money in the canteens on Sabbath, thus soldiers who do not have coupons are not served, etc.

'The Anatomy and Pathology Law' (1953), which was formulated with the active cooperation of rabbinical circles and religious physicians, and which, despite its restrictions, was considered as satisfactory also by the medical profession and the juridical authorities, is one of those laws whose change, intended to impose extreme restrictions, is aggressively demanded by the Orthodox. Were it not for the energetic opposition of the doctors, the coalitionary government would almost certainly have already approved and passed it.

In the first five paragraphs of this law, rules are laid down specifying the conditions under which a deceased may be transferred for a post mortem examination for purposes of medical study. Since it concerned those deceased whose bodies were *not* requested by their families, no public problems arose until the Ministry of Religious Affairs interfered with a directive that *every* deceased Jew had to be buried at its expense. From that time on, there was continual interference and obstruction by the Chevroth Kadisha (burial societies) who demanded the body of every deceased Jew; and in particular the theme of post mortems has become a subject not only of political controversy and bargaining, but also of periodic rioting by the ultra-orthodox circles and the emergence of a society with the exclusive aim of fighting for the total prohibition of post mortem examination. The problem of post mortem examination (the archaic taboo is based on the belief that the body must be intact at the Messianic Time of the resurrection of the dead) played a unique role even before the establishment of the State. Because of Orhodox pressure, there was no anatomy taught at the Hebrew University of Jerusalem for many years, so that medical students were obliged to study abroad for the first two years of their curriculum.

The law prohibiting pig breeding (1962) and restricting it to non-Jewish villages has a somewhat shorter, but no less dramatic history. Since the establishment of the State, governmental and municipal authorities, under various pretexts and by illegal measures (as stated by the Supreme Court) have attempted to hinder and even prevent pig breeding (and selling) by Jews. Finally, in 1962 Mapai accepted this coalitionary condition of the Orthodox, and the ridiculous and anti-democratic law was passed.

Characteristic are the rules, fixed by the (Orthodox) Minister of Interior, regarding the destruction of illegally bred or transported confiscated pigs:

'The inspector will order the destruction of the pigs confiscated according to Ordinance 4 in one of the following ways, provided it does not cause public nuisance: 1) burning; 2) burial in earth; 3) drowning in the sea; 4) transfer for feeding animals and birds in public gardens or transfer to scientific and research institutes for experimental study and research'.

I know of no case where the provision of Point 4 was applied. The barbaric method of destroying the animals reminds one of the deeds of the victorious Crusader, who, after defeating his *satanic* enemy, annihilates the remains so that no trace of the unholy should contaminate the sacred soil of the (sacred) nation.

'The Legal Competence and Guardianship Law, 1962' has purely social and humanitarian aims, providing protection to the child against incapable and irresponsible parents. However, in its abusive execution, it also provides opportunity for Orthodox activists of the Ministry of Social Affairs to disqualify (by Court order) parents who dare to educate their children in non-Jewish boarding schools.

It is not possible to enumerate here all the municipal by-laws of the different localities (the legality of which is often highly questionable) relating to religious coercion. Most of these enforce kashruth and Sabbath observance (supplementing, in this way, the 'Law of Work and Rest Hours' by further restrictions). Apart from interfering in the citizen's private life, by-laws enforcing Sabbath observance (prohibition of theatre performances, etc.) have a special significance from a social and public (mental) health point of view: because of the lunar Hebrew calendar, Sabbath starts on Friday evening, so instead of going to the cinema, etc., on the eve of the day of rest (as do people in most countries) in Israel one goes there at the end - starting the week in an unrelaxed condition.

The social, psychological and health aspects of this and also the fact that, due to the closing of movies, clubs and similar places, the only possible entertainment for the youth is in the street or private parties, require a special study.

III. Similar to the laws of personal status, these laws have a discriminatory effect on the minority and result in a feeling of inequality and of being a second rate citizen. This has a detrimental social effect and partially determines the Jewish-Arab relationship.

Apart from the previously mentioned religious laws, which are also coercive concerning the non-Jewish population of the State and the fact that Arabs are not called up to military service - which is surely a formal rather than real discrimination - the legal basis for the discrimination against the minorities is given under five laws and ordinances: the 'Emergency Regulations, 1945'; the 'Absentee Property Law, 1951'; the 'Citizenship Law, 1952'; the discriminatory execution of the 'Land Acquisition (Validation of Operations and Compensations) Law, 1953' and the 'Local Authorities Ordinance' (the last providing equal opportunity to exert political pressure on the Jewish population).

A full appraisal of the effects and influences of these laws is not yet available. It would be totally naive to deny that a prominent part of the minority population has a hostile attitude towards the State (which is, however, quite naturally, enhanced by these same laws). It would be equally naive to accept without reservation the official version - that all the restrictions are based exclusively on security considerations. The question of the sequestered Arab lands, again, in its social, economic and psychological ramifications and influences is so vast a concept that all aspects of this subject require extensive treatment. For instance, the transformation of a considerable part of the *fellahim* into urban (sub)-proletarians linked (but not integrated) to the Jewish towns, enjoying, on the one hand, the economic boom of Israeli society at large, but at the same time, being victims of social (instead of the former legal) discrimination. For instance, when a high-salaried Arab worker finds it impossible to lease a room in Tel Aviv; or a situation in which the economic recession hits them first, causing them to reflux to the villages, become unemployed and uprooted persons, etc. A special theme is the psychological reaction and understandable feeling of bitterness of a former owner of an expropriated parcel of land which is allocated to a Jewish kibbutz or individual. Another problem is the often contradictory attitude of the authorities - characterized, on the one hand by a sincere wish to develop the Arab villages (by regrouping to form larger areas to enable intensive cultivation) and, on the other, by hostility and greediness (generally paying inadequate compensation to former owners). Frequently, Israeli goodwill, animosity and incompetence are intermingled, while Arab suspicions, well-founded or in some cases totally unfounded, exist. The complexity of the subject leaves us no choice but to refer the reader to the relevant literature, and to restrict ourselves to a few remarks:

Two basically erraneous opinions (misinterpretations) are ingrained in the Israeli (Jewish) public when discussing or contemplating the Arab problem resulting from the restrictions and suffering imposed on the Arabs as a consequence of the 1948 war. These are the restrictions of movement that require most residents to obtain a permit from the Military Governor to leave their localities; this is the sole discriminatory measure (having no further practical consequences), but it causes oversensitivity on the part of the minorities. The term 'refugee' (or 'absentee') covers only those Arabs who are outside the boundaries of the State.

The practical restrictions of freedom of movement are per se only part, although an important one, of the possible discriminations. Equally important is the feeling of being a second-class citizen at the mercy of the Military Governor and his officials, whose powers are almost unlimited the moment he justifies any of his decisions for security reasons. This is more so since security consideration is a subject which the Supreme Court refrains from deliberating, though it has voiced doubts as to the sincerity of some of the justifications brought forth by the Defense Authorities.

There is not the least doubt that in many cases the security considerations related by the authorities are well founded. But it is equally certain that in other instances they are purely fictitious, as, for instance, if an Arab student is suddenly, for 'security reasons', prevented from returning to University in Jerusalem, to sit his examinations, or when opposition politicians are confined by administrative order to their villages prior to attending a political meeting - and the next day the 'security reasons' cease to exist. The fact that (Jewish) political parties, extremely sensitive on security matters (such as 'Herut' and 'Ahdut Haavoda') also affirm that the Military Government does not serve the security of the State, but rather, the interests of the ruling party, confirms the above-mentioned doubts.

The variety of objective and arbitrary reasons and executions typical of the area of security matters, also characterizes the practical execution of the law concerning land expropriation.

The feeling of arbitrariness is necessarily augmented by the fact that, according to paragraph 28 of the 'Absentee Property Law', the Custodian is entitled to release part of the properties *at his discretion;* and if the complaint of many Arab residents is true, then only those who 'vote as one should at the elections' can hope to regain their land, while the fate of the others is poverty and distress.

Sometimes, the decisions of the Minister of Interior are equally discriminatory, on religious grounds. For example, in the case of the village of Kafr Yassif, whose *elected* council members were not docile enough, he changed the status of the village in order to be able to *appoint* people who would be more 'cooperative' and willing to prohibit pig breeding. (His decision was annulled by the Supreme Court).

The far-reaching liberalization of the restrictions on the movement of the Arab population when there was a marked shortage of unskilled labour in the towns and also the fact that the remaining restrictions make possible the economic exploitation of Arab workers are additional arguments that security considerations were partly, but probably not the only reason for the unchanged maintenance of the Draconic Emergency Regulations dating from 1945.

Concerning these regulations, enacted by the Mandatory Government in order to fight the activities of the *Jewish national movement,* Arab authors never fail to cite texts of prominent Jewish lawyers (some of whom are today among Israel's leading personalities) who once, in the harshest possible words, criticized those same regulations denouncing them as unworthy of a civilized country.

Only future historians will be able to decide whether or not Arabs, and perhaps also Jews, were unjustly treated and abused on the basis of those regulations.

What is unquestionable is that some of the measures executed by the military authorities were brutally discriminatory and cynical deeds, leaving deep wounds in the souls of the local Arabs.

Laws which make the Arab citizens a legally discriminated minority will remain a crucial element in the apartheid like co-existence of the two nations (though *socially* this situation precedes the emergence of the State) and the feeling of living in a hostile state.

This is especially true for Arab intellectuals who, contrary to another stratum of the population, did not benefit, either economically or regarding social status, from the economic affluence of the early sixties, and the great majority of whom did not accede to positions to which their professional competence entitled them. It is illusory to speak about equality as long as Arab writers are forced to break off a meeting with their Jewish colleagues in order to be able to return at a prescribed hour to their localities, or when a representative of the authorities in the 'Triangle' can decide, at his discretion, that some villager may travel to physician A in Nethanya and not to B, in Hadera.

All this, taking into consideration the heated nationalist atmosphere (on both Jewish and Arab sides), does not mean that otherwise the attitude of the Arabs towards the State would be a positive one; but until such laws cease to exist, one cannot even hope for a change in attitude and a vicious circle is thus created.

On the other hand, the knowledge that their Arab fellow-citizen is discriminated against and in some aspects, defenseless, has a *corrupting* effect on the Jewish population. This is primarily true for those primitive elements who are in everyday contact with them, since their attitude is based not only on the feeling of *strength* of the majority, but also on feelings of *superiority* towards the 'inferior' and defenseless. Such a boastful attitude breeds not only racist feelings and ideas, but falsifies the whole perspective of Israeli-Arab relations, creating the illusion that the Arab states are similarly 'inferior' and defenseless, as are the local minority. The axiom of the solution to the Israeli-Arab problems will, in their eyes, conform to the 'wisdom based on life experience' (a 'wisdom' pre-existing to the actual conflict): 'I know the Arabs well; they are all cowards and treacherous. A kick in the teeth is the only language they understand'.

IV. Finally, some laws and projected laws which are contrary to the freedom of the individual, and, on the other hand, some projected laws with a humanitarian and democratic aim, have to be mentioned in this context. The passage of some of these laws, or the prevention of the enactment of some of the projected laws, the amendments and discussions prior to their passage, are highly illustrative of the social dynamism and conflict of diverging interests, and especially those of the ruling circles in present-day Israel.

The following laws belong in this category: 'Amendment to the Penal Code (Security of the State) 1957'; the 'Libel Law, 1965'; the 'Foreign Travel Tax Law'; the 'Law of Compulsory Organization-Fees of Workers, 1964'; some retroactive laws (which, with very few exceptions, by their being retroactive violate a basic principle of the Rule of Law) and some of the projected laws (partly already having their first reading in the Knesset) such as the 'Sabbath Law'; the amendment to the 'Anatomy and Pathology Law', the Amendments to the 'Register of Residents Ordinance, 1948' and the 'Cooperative Societies Ordinance'. On the other hand, the rejected projected laws aiming at the abolishment of the Military Government, or that enabling the contract of civil marriage for persons who want it; another which would make possible at least civil divorce for those couples one of whom is a foreign citizen, and still another aiming at the abolition of the 'mohar'; a projected law which was intended to replace an outdated one which makes homosexuality a severe criminal offense; another proposing an arrangement based on humanitarian and social considerations for cases of artificial abortion; and finally, respective Bills of Human Rights proposed by Prof. Klinghoffer and Prof. Akzin, and a projected law with similar aims by U. Avneri.

One Draconic regulation contrary to the democratic principles of the Rule of Law is paragraph 24 of the Amended Penal Code, which aroused public storm and heated controversy, when, in connection with the trial of the noted historian, A. Cohen, one of the judges of the Supreme Court observed the absurdity of some of its phrasings. In its present form, it is up to the accused to prove his innocence, and not up to the prosecution to prove the guilt of a person who had 'unauthorized contact with a foreign agent', because he is automatically supposed to have passed secret information, while neither the concept of a 'foreign agent' nor that of 'secret information' is adequately defined. So, theoretically, any social contact with a foreign diplomat could result in an accusation; or if, say, a sociologist lecturing at an international scientific congress, had passed the 'secret' information that there was dissatisfaction in Israeli professional circles because of the custom which ensures high-ranking officers of directorial posts in public institutions and enterprises after their discharge.

Some years ago, the Minister of Justice proposed a change in paragraph 24, satisfactory at least insofar that the prosecution will have to prove that the accused was aware, or should have been aware, that he was meeting a foreign agent, but as to the crucial point of the 'passing of secret information' no essential improvement is proposed.

The Libel Law (enacted in 1965) which replaced an older one and which, according to its critics was introduced solely because some libel trials ended very unsatisfactorily for the Government is also one of the laws with a stormy history, underwent modifications and is presently subject to amendments. The first draft of this law included such severe provisions which threatened not only the freedom of the press but also the normal principles of judicial procedures (prohibiting papers from reporting on the happenings in libel trials) that the Supreme Court saw it necessary to draw the attention of the Government to the grave consequences involved in the proposed law. Although some of the planned provisions were dropped, such as the abovementioned prohibition, and the proposed punishment for defamation of the State (where does the 'State' end and where does the *regime* begin? And where does criticism end and defamation begin?), etc., while others which were aimed at political opponents backfired. The present more liberal form of the law is restrictive enough to hamper free criticism; especially the provision that proof of the truth of the incriminated statement is not enough to be a 'good defense', but that it must be proven that it was in the public interest that the news should be published and in the *form* in which it was done.

The following laws have a common factor-interference with the freedom of movement of the citizen, contradicting at least the spirit if not always the letter of paragraph XIII.2 of the Declaration of Human Rights.

The foreign travel tax (in some cases higher than the price of the travel ticket) is officially justified for fiscal reasons; however, it is even more an expression of the hostile attitude against 'unpatriotic' and 'snobbish' tendencies to travel abroad. The fact that even an English teacher who travels to England in order to enlarge his professional knowledge, a scientist who participates in an international congress, or a university student who visits foreign countries during his vacations, has to pay this 'luxury' tax, severely hampers the acquisition of necessary knowledge. The anti-democratic character of this law is especially striking in view of the energetic demand of Israel that no difficulties should prevent any Jew wishing to leave his country in order to emigrate to Israel. A cartoon in one of the papers depicted a Soviet diplomat saying to an Israeli: 'You too do not let them go out?' stressed this fact in a witty way. I do not intend to compare the factual situation in the two countries; especially in the sixties, tens of thousands of Israelis travel each year, individually and in organized tours, but the enforcement of this law is symptomatic of the spirit of the administration in its disregard for civil rights.

Equally restrictive is the 'Passports Law' (amended 1965) empowering the Minister of Interior to withdraw the passport of an Israeli living abroad, and to refuse (at his own discretion!) to issue one for reasons 'detrimental to the interests of the State', while another law empowers him not to consent to the wish of a citizen living abroad to renounce his citizenship.

The planned law of 'Compulsory Service of Physicians in Border Areas', obliging every physician to serve after finishing his studies in the border area, and prohibiting him from leaving the country without special permission during the years of his studies and the following three years, violates not only freedom of movement, but also that of the choice of one's working place in time of peace.

The above projected law, as well as the following, and also the law obliging unorganized workers to pay trade union duties, reveal the tendency of granting near dictatorial rights to *political-bureaucratic machineries* (of the Workers Sick Fund, the Secretariat of the Moshav Movement and the Histadrut) denying the principle of freedom of *voluntary* membership in organizational frameworks.

The proposed so-called 'Moshav Law' (part of the broader 'Cooperative Societies Ordinance) is particularly autocratic, granting authority to the central bureaucratic apparatus to remove a member of a moshav (also on political or religious grounds!) or to interfere with his right to bequeath his property according to his wishes; moreover denying even his right to appeal to a state court against decisions of forums of the movement, thus turning him into a legally deprived citizen, and contradicting every principle of the Rule of Law.

Of special importance is the law of the Register of Residents, its goal being the undoing of the consequences of a Supreme Court ruling denying the clerk of this office the right to conduct inquiries, and restricting his function to the registration of data brought before him; a judgment which forced the Ministry to register as married a mixed couple, married abroad in civil marriage. The aim of the Orthodox parties was to empower the clerk to turn, in cases of doubt, to *rabbinical authorities* (who would, of course, rule in every case of personal status according to the Halacha) and in this way close the gap which gives the citizen a legal loophole for evading theocratic regulation of his status. Though the law as passed in 1965 was somewhat watered down and some provisions were left for future decision, but even so, it makes things more difficult for the citizen (e.g. in declaring that he is without religion).

The (disguised) 'Sabbath Law', again, if accepted in its unmodified form, will cause not only further restrictions (its proposed prohibitions now encompass not only employees, but also activities of self-employed persons, invading their strict privacy; e.g., a lawyer may be punished if he writes a letter in his office) but it also discriminates between the kibbutzim (where the provisions are more lenient), the rest of the population and also religious minorities.

The following humanitarian laws were rejected following Orthodox pressure: E. Salmi proposed a civil marriage contract; the Minister of Justice made it possible for a civil divorce to be granted to couples, one of whom is a foreign citizen (two successive presidents of the Supreme Court, Olshan and Agranat drew attention to the absurd situation which did not allow for divorce); the revision of outdated laws concerning homosexual relations between consenting adults (punishable, according to the Bible, by death!) and concerning artificial abortion [5]. The last law was also opposed by some secularist nationalists who, for example, are as Ben Gurion, obsessed by the idea of increasing the natality of the Jewish people.

The proposition put forward by U. Avneri to give constitutional legal power to the principles expressed in the Charter of Independence was also rejected by representatives of both the religious and secularist parties, whose machineries are equally afraid of the enactment of constitutional rights, since they may interfere with their semi-totalitarian rule (6).

Summing up the subject of the legal sources of prejudices and discrimination in Israel and expressing some hope for future developments in this field, the following can be said:

1. There is very little chance that precisely the law which we denoted as the most reactionary (that of personal status, marriage and divorce) will be changed, unless external influences prevail. The reason is the almost complete opposition of the Orthodox defenders of theocracy, but it is also due to the character and ideology of the old-time ruling class and its conviction that religion strengthens the unity of the nation. I insist, in different parts of this book, on the predominant falsity of this argument, and will not repeat those refutations here. It seems that only external pressure (either by American Jewry, or on the part of some of the forums of the U.N.) may lead to a radical change and to the abolition of the exclusive validity of the existing religious-racist laws.

5. In practically both fields a very liberal and humanistic attitude prevails in Israel; or at least it was so until a short time ago. The former State Attorney (today Justice) C. Cohen instructed the police to close files after the first inquiry, and the same was the practice during the office of his successor, G. Hausner. The State Attorney, Ben-Zeev, revoked those instructions, but for the time being, no practical changes are noted. The change coincided with the replacement of P. Rosen as Minister of Justice (during whose term in office, this Ministry was perhaps the only one which was not an instrument of party manoeuvres) by D. Joseph, who also cancelled the autonomy of the State Attorney - in spite of the opinion expressed by judges of the Supreme Court.

2. One can expect a gradual liberalization in the field of discriminatory laws oppressing the Arab minority, unless dramatic military-political events occur. But as long as the Absentee Property Law is not changed (concerning the 'present absentees' and a fair compensation for expropriated land), it will poison the relations of the two nations of the country.

3. Because of the sociological nature of the ruling class, one has to expect that the regime will continue to pass laws which aim the strengthening of the power of the executive authority, and will pay further coalitionary 'dues' to the Orthodox partner attempting thus to create a form of *legalized semitotalitarian rule* of the administration.

Prof. Akzin was correct in his statement:

'The struggle for or against individual rights or the States' powers tends to become a mere incident in the Opposition's attack on Ministers and in the Coalition's defense of them, with the consequent unwillingness of Coalition members to risk weakening the Cabinet, and the reduction of chances of Opposition members to break the serried ranks of purposeful majority, whatever the merits of the case.' (1)

Contrary to this, his prediction in the same lecture, that secular forces will gradually overbear, did not materialize. Since 1956, religious coercive laws, regulations and instructions have become more and more oppressive.

4. If the regime encounters sharp opposition by public bodies (as in the case of the first draft of the Libel Law or that of the Anatomy and Pathology Law) it tends to (temporarily) withdraw - not so much due to a sincere persuasion of the necessity to renounce undemocratic legislation, but as a surrender to pressure groups or to attain its aims by devious means (the Law of Moshavim, the 'Sabbath Law').

From the point of view of the shaping of the physiognomy of the Israeli State and society, in our opinion, the principal task of democrats and opponents of theocracy and racism is the fight against the laws governing personal status, marriage and divorce. The struggle against these inhumane and antisocial regulations by *all* possible means is morally justified, since a regime which passes laws contradicting basic human rights outlaws itself.

BIBLIOGRAPHY [6]

1. AKZIN, B.: Constitutional and Administrative Law (Int. Conv. of Lawyers in Israel, 1958) Jerusalem.
2. ALONI, S.: The Rights of the Child in the State of Israel (Tarbut Vhinuh, Tel Aviv, 1964).
3. BEN MENASHE, J.: Freedom of Conscience in Issues of Personal Status ('Lamerhav', 17.2.1963).
4. HAUSNER, G.: Individual's Rights in Courts (Int. Conv. of Lawyers in Israel, 1958, Jerusalem).
5. TALMON, J.: 'Who is a Jew?', Encounter, May 1965.
6. TAMARIN, G. R.: The Israeli Dilemma - Ghetto State or Free Society? (B. Lessin Lecture, Tel Aviv, 1965) (Chapter 1 of this book).
7. UNITED NATIONS Report on the Main Types and Causes of Discrimination, New York, 1949, 1965, 1967.

6. Titles 2, 3, and 6 are Hebrew texts.

3. Non-legal forms of prejudice and discrimination *

We will confine our rabbis to their synagogues and our officers to their barracks.

Th. Herzl, 'The State of the Jews'

More than the Jews observed the Sabbath, the Sabbath safeguarded them.

A. Haam, 'On the Crossroad'

The Lord, He should be blessed, did not impose tyranny on his creatures.

Avodah Zara 3a

---

* From: 'Forms and Foundations of Israeli Theocracy', Shikpul Press, Tel Aviv, 1968.

I. The subject of this chapter is restricted to a single theme, to the dominant aspect in the field of prejudice and discrimination in Israel - religious coercion. Other domains of non-legal and sometimes outrightly illegal discriminatory treatment of the minorities, will be dealt with in the chapters on Jewish-Arab relations. In comparison the phenomena of prejudice and discrimination in other areas, such as in (Jewish) intercommunity relations or those based on political motives (eg. discrimination against leftwingers in the Army and some public institutions, etc.) are of far less importance.

When speaking about non-legalized forms of religious coercion in everyday life one deals with a multivarious and *fluid* realm, which is meant in more than one sense.

Some aspects of religious coercion are permanent and generalized (eg. closing ports on the Sabbath, forcing all patients and medical personnel to eat kosher in the hospitals, pressure on parents to remove their children from church-owned schools, etc.). In other fields, the situation changes not only from place to place, but also according to momentary coalitionary agreements and actual power-relations in the government or one or other municipality. Furthermore, a given practice (eg. of some municipality) which was clearly unlawful until a certain date, may overnight become legal due to a new (sometimes retroactive) law, not to mention that the limits of legal and illegal are in some cases rather dubious, since the rights of some religious bodies (eg. of the Caraite Religious Council) are ambiguous or not at all defined. Sometimes privately expressed opinions of religious officials which are not legally binding, become so, since they are simultaneously state employees while some manoeuvres of a public body aiming at the enforcement of religious practices indirectly make the citizen a transgressor of a non-religious regulation. [1]

The following examples illustrate what has just been stated: in Haifa there is an almost regular bus service on the Sabbath, which is not the case in Tel Aviv (even the escalators of the underground stop); in Bnei Brak and some quarters of Jerusalem the driver who dares to enter, will most probably be attacked by stone-throwing fanatics. In most of the non-religious kibbutzim a member is free from any interference of ritualistic dietary laws but their pig breeding branches were mostly abolished

---

1. For instance, some municipalities (although not forbidding bathing on their beaches on New Year's Day) suspend the services of the life savers, thus hindering many would-be bathers, while making the others (sometimes thousands) automatically transgressors, since bathing is forbidden where there are no life savers.

after prohibition became legally binding. The citizen of the big cities, who (until recently) could send an express letter also on Sabbath, now finds the notice: *On Sabbath and Jewish holidays the post maintains only telegraphic service.* In Nahariya, Tivon, some of the kibbutzim, and in some quarters of the big cities, a couple of mixed marriage can live happily without ever encountering animosity, but if they move only a few kilometers away their life (and even that of their children) may become hell.

Notwithstanding all possible minor differences, one has immediately to point out the most striking, typical and common trait of religious coercion in Israel - its *public* character.

An example of this is the *absence* of statues in the squares of the cities, the *presence* of mezuzoth even on the doors of laboratories of scientific institutes, the placard announcing that smoking is forbidden on the Sabbath in the dining rooms of rest houses (hospitals, etc.), the fact that even the dogs of the Police Force are fed on rice (not bread) during Passover and the practice of changing the blue license plates on the cars of ministers to ordinary yellow ones on the Sabbath so that they will desecrate the Sabbath as private persons - not in their official capacity.

This is precisely the outstanding feature of Israeli religious coercion - while in secular regimes it is axiomatic that religion is *a private issue of the citizen; the state being neutral in this matter.* In Israel, the opposite is true. In most areas of his private life, the citizen is (for the time being!) free to remain as remote from religious observance as it pleases him, but in the public realm theocratic practices drastically curtail his liberties.

In this context, it is even superfluous to stress the total arbitrariness of many of the definitions of public (versus private) places (or enterprises) - as, for example, why should the dining room of a ship be more public than the deck, or what makes sherut-taxis less public than a bus cooperative? The characteristic feature, however, is that the moment something *is* labelled or considered public - religious coercion is applied.

And this is exactly the goal of the Orthodox, the realm they intend to dominate; in which, according to ancient mores, they are commanded to enforce the laws of the Torah. They will not interfere with someone smoking on the Sabbath, provided it is not in a public place, or with someone driving his private car but they fight without compromise to achieve the prohibition of any form of public transportation, in order to give the '*parhesia*' (public realm, community life) a 'Jewish character'.

To justify religious coercion in its legal and non-legalized forms, the following arguments are constantly put forward:

a. 'Israel is a *Jewish* state and it is necessary that its public realm should have a Jewish coloration', which again, is per force a religious coloration. 'Our way is not that of all the peoples, the Israeli Sabbath should not be a simple day of rest, as in other nations, but a special sanctified day.'
b. It is wrong to speak about religious coercion after the coalition majority have enacted some legislative regulation, since democracy means the rule of the majority.
c. It is not coercion at all, since the secularists are *not commanded* by their religion to eat *non kosher; not to travel on the Sabbath*, etc.
d. Every law means coercion of some kind, and there is no difference at all between a law forcing a citizen to pay taxes or serve in the army, and another which forces him to get married by a rabbi or prohibits some infraction of religious customs. (An argument heard sometimes even by liberal professional politicians.)
e. An additional, constantly repeated argument in favor of religious coercion, in whatever form it may appear is: It was religion, with its restrictive practices (segregatory marriage laws, kashrut, etc.) which, for thousands of years, safeguarded the Jewish people from assimilation into other nations.

Few people in Israel would even dream of posing in this context the question, whether *every price* should be paid for the maintenance of Jewry as a separate entity (including the price of intolerance and lack of freedom of conscience (especially in an age of general progressive decline in the significance of organized religion) or whether the moral justification of a particularist existence would not be seriously invalidated if it has to be maintained by coercion, racialism and segregation?

As to the first point of the above arguments (and even disregarding the fact that Israel is not an *exclusively* Jewish state) the following clarifications are pertinent:

a. The request for a specific Jewish 'coloration' should not be interpreted as local color in the superficial sense as used by tourists.
b. When arguing for the continuance of religious values and tradition with the specific 'flavour' its proponents fail to mention the fact that all these habits and prohibitions are today expressions of the *Orthodox* Jewish way of life. But for the Orthodox *their* style and conception of religion is the only valid Judaism. They will reluctantly admit, if pressed, that the habits, for instance, of Reform Judaism are very different indeed, but they have a simple argument which is sufficient

to prevent any further discussion: reform leads to assimilation (and maybe even to conversion) and thus its way of life and ideology are eo ipso branded as treacherous and automatically disqualified. Knowing that for the Israeli chauvinists assimilation is the most *abject crime,* the orthodox activists have the intuitive conviction that Reformist mores and rights can be dismissed without much ado.

The fallacy of the other propositions is evident to anyone who grew up in a democratic society; coercion, of course, means not only prevention of religious practices but equally the interference with basic rights to *do* something: democracy means not *only* ruling by the majority but also safeguarding of the undeniable rights of the *individual,* which should not be violated by any kind of coercive legislation. It is also clear that there *is* an enormous difference between compulsory payment of taxes (for purposes which are common to the vast majority of the population, e.g. building roads), and enforcing an observance of values which may be of no value at all for a section of the population, in the name of a God whose existence the citizen perhaps does not believe in. (True, every state has regulations concerning marriage ceremonies, nevertheless the Orthodox 'forget' that the *content* of the Israeli ones means a scandalous violation of the basic rights laid down in the Declaration of Human Rights.) Religious coercion oppresses the secular citizen from birth until death and subsequently his descendants. The following are examples of this chronology.

CIRCUMCISION - VOLUNTARY AND INVOLUNTARY

In the first days of life the newborn citizen and his parents are free from any religious coercion. The Social Security provides hospital care and maternity benefit. Infant mortality in Israel is among the lowest in the world.

If the baby is a boy, the mother will be presented on the second or third day with the visiting card of the *mochel* who is linked to the hospital. If no arrangements are made immediately for the *brith mila,* he will return day after day.

The number of Israelis who have the operation performed by a physician and without religious ceremony - including the habit of sucking the wound - is insignificant (only a few intellectuals). The invitation of friends and neighbours to the ceremony is a strict social obligation and in a petite bourgeoisie society, very few dare to risk the contempt of neighbours and colleagues.

No Israeli parents, irreligious they may be, would dream of not having their sons circumcised. They will, sensibly, not risk persecution of the child by his peers because of the ideology of his parents.

Serious problems concerning circumcision sometimes arise in connection with young uncircumcised European migrants, whose parents decided not to circumcise them either on ideological grounds or because of deeply traumatic memories, related to World War II, when many Jews living under false names were identified as Jews and killed because of the mark of the Brith Mila.

A further possible problem is posed by the fact that any surgical intervention in the genital area may cause or activate neurotic fears. The psychologist or psychiatrist who is consulted by the parents about this subject is in a rather difficult dilemma to decide between two unfavorable choices: to risk the possible neurotic complications if he recommends the operation, or if he opposes it, to expose the boy to the danger of becoming an outcast.

In the great majority of cases, the youngster consents to be circumcized and often requests the operation. But there are also cases of categorical refusal both by the boy and his parents.

A public and moral aspect of the problem is that according to secret instructions given to all Youth Aliya institutions, every youngster is to be expelled from the institutions if, one year after his arrival, he still refuses to be circumcized.

The following was said by Mrs. A., head of a school in a kibbutz of Hashomer Hazair:

'We do not conceal from our children that it is a religious ritual and that we undergo it not to be different from the rest of the nation. We are linked to a Mochel, since it would be too cumbersome and expensive to call a physician every time. There is also the problem of the grandparents. Some of them categorically insist that the ceremony should be done according to tradition. There were problems with boys coming from Poland. We did explain to our children that many of these boys were not circumcised. It is true, they behaved rather badly towards these boys, calling them 'Goy'. Personally, I can remember five youngsters; three of them requested the operation before enlisting in the Army; two refused. As to the instructions from Aliyot Noar? They have tried to deny that such instructions were given, but I have a letter signed by Mr. K. himself; the instructions are clearcut.'

On the same subject Mr. L, a religious, but very liberal-minded teacher, who immigrated from a Maghrebian country had the following to say:

'In our communities, though predominantly traditionalist, the approach to religious matters was much more tolerant. I was very much astonished, although I am personally deeply religious, when in the Army, we learned that the orderly had orders to report, after each VD inspection, about the uncircumcised soldiers. They were then called before the CO; subsequently, most of them consented to being circumcised.'

FREE AND SECULAR EDUCATION?

The influence of the educational curriculum as a source of religious and nationalist prejudices will be treated in a special chapter VII of this book.

Some examples of unlawful religious coercion in the public state schools are presented. These phenomena are usually initiated by the head of a municipal education department, the director of a school, or some of the teachers, generally tacitly endorsed by the educational authorities.

From time to time, papers report on mutual complaints in secular and religious circles regarding dishonest methods or pressure put on parents to register their children either in the school belonging to the general or to the religious trend. In most cases, the grievances of both parties are well-founded. In the first years after the establishment of the State, there were cases of anti-religious coercion, especially among new immigrants, while today the reverse is true. Political activists do their utmost to influence parents to register their children in the school of their 'allegiance', since indirectly, party influence can be exerted. In new settlements a common slogan of the orthodox activists against schools of the general trend is: 'Do not enroll your child in the school of the apostates.'

The curriculum of the general trend formally contains neither the subject 'Religion' (although the study of the Bible, in a traditionalist way is the central discipline) nor any obligation to pray or conform with religious practices. Nevertheless in recent years, knowledge of some of the prayers is required at the matriculation examination, and, for example, the list of prerequisites for the boarding school at the Pardess Hannah Agricultural school contains a prayer book. In many schools, boys are requested to wear skullcaps during the Bible hour.

Most parents accept this without protest. But some refuse to comply.

When Yaakov was in the second class (in a school in South Tel Aviv) - reports Mrs. H., the wife of a high-ranking official - he came home one day relating the request of the teacher to bring a skullcap tomorrow, since they will start the study of the Bible. I told him that he will wear no skullcap and nobody can force him to do so. The next day I got an invitation to the Director (an activist of Mapai).

Why does it bother you if the child wears a skullcap when all the other children do so?

I told him that he will wear one if he can show me a formal precept of the Ministry of Education.

He answered: Why do you have to make him different from the rest of the class? ...But he did not insist any more.

There were only four children out of forty (the parents were Mapam members) who dared to complain and did not acquiesce to the request.

A special realm of social pressure (sometimes public and even semi-official) concerns Jewish children studying in schools owned by one of the churches. While the State painstakingly tries to safeguard the rights of the religious minorities, anything even remotely reminiscent of missionary activities evokes almost paranoid reactions. This is particularly true for the Orthodox circles but they also succeeded in inducing an oversensitivity in the public at large, as if a wide scale conspiracy by missionaries exists to convert Israel's Jews. This reaction is indicative of the days of the European Middle Ages, when the Christian *majority* tried to convert the Jewish minority living in its midst, and not the reality of a country with an insignificant Christian population living within a Jewish majority. Characteristic of this oversensitivity are the following examples: the Hebrew University decided to remove a group of statues representing Moses, Jesus and Mohammed donated by a famous sculptor, because of the angry reaction of some Orthodox professors. The trustees of the Mann Auditorium in Tel Aviv refused to accept the donation of an organ, since some of the spectators would be reminded of a church; the directors of Kol Israel felt obliged to explain why it permitted Prof. Flusser to mention the life of Jesus (which might have a missionary influence!) in a talk about the significance of Galilee.

After the persistent request of the Orthodox to ban missionary activities by legislation, the government conducted a survey which revealed that from the time of the establishment of the state, only a few hundred Jews converted to Christianity, most of them while preparing for emigration. During the same period, thousands of Christian spouses were converted to Judaism, not so much out of conviction, but due to environmental pressure.

There are certainly some Christian institutions (mostly belonging to the smaller Protestant sects) whose principal aim is to convert, but there are others who are not interested in proselytising. Jewish parents who send their children to schools owned by one of the churches (mostly to

French convents, since the standard of teaching there is high and the matriculation certificate is recognized by the French government), can be divided *grosso modo* into three categories: parents from Central and Western European countries, dissatisfied with the low standard of general education at the Israeli public schools and whose principal aim is that the children should master foreign languages and receive a broad education; parents from countries of French culture (predominantly from North Africa, sometimes very religious people) for whose children study in French means a natural continuation of the previous studies and for many (since at 18 they must enlist in the Army) the only possibility to obtain their matriculation certificate; and finally, socially-deprived parents from different countries of origin, for whom the possibility of placing their children in a boarding school is extremely attractive.

Orthodox propaganda presents the facts as if all cases were those of the third category. This version, as said before, permeated the mind of the public at large.

The author encountered this problem for the first time some 15 years ago. One day, an elderly cleaning woman in his hospital department turned to him very perplexed, asking for advice. The day before, one of the Ministers, hospitalized in a neighboring department, asked her, the new immigrant, with very sincere interest and sympathy, about the conditions of the absorption of her family. She told him, among other things, that her 18 year old son was studying in the last grade of the St. Joseph School, and since he was a good student in Egypt (who interrupted his studies in the last class when they immigrated) she hoped that he would soon get his matriculation certificate. He censured her severely for giving him 'into the hands of foreigners'. My reassurance, stating that in the given circumstances, she did the right thing, sufficed to calm her; I doubt if today things would be so simple.

Two short fragments of conversations with a student and a rejected candidate serve to illustrate the state of affairs.

Mrs. P.: 'After sending my application for admission, I was invited to an interview with Dr. L., a lecturer. Her questions were about my previous studies and the relationship to religious tradition at home. I had the impression that all was O.K. But I was off guard when she asked: 'Well, but how will you finish your studies if you become pregnant one day?' and I answered spontaneously that this will not happen before I get my degree. This was enough to reject me.'

Mr. Z.: 'I said openly that I am not religious, and was rejected. Then, my mother remembered Rabbi X, and he gave her a letter of recommendation stating that although I am not religious, my mother is from a family of famous rabbis and she can influence me. I was accepted.

The affair of my two expelled colleagues? Simply bad luck. Another student informed the authorities that they had been eating bread on Passover; the next day they were expelled.'

TWO FACES OF KASHRUTH - PURE AND IMPURE FANATICISM

Archaic alimentary taboos, especially those concerning separation between milk and meat and the regulations of ritual slaughter, are shaping many aspects of the everyday life of the Israeli citizen. From the point of view of the non-religious, these regulations mean an unwarranted and most unpleasant interference in his private life and also a ransom extracted from him in the form of a higher price for the meat he eats, the wine he drinks, the hotel room he sleeps in, etc. In certain professions, there is an obligation to pay exorbitant sums to the monopolists of kashruth-certificates. From the point of view of the Orthodox, this aspect of Israeli reality represents a way of life which is in accordance with their beliefs, and it is natural that the secularists also have to pay the price for it (in the financial sense, as well as the restriction of their freedom). Also related to the laws of dietary purity, one meets phenomena where the most *pure* and *impure* forms of fanaticism are constantly intermingled. This means that the religious authorities manifest only pure fanaticism, in both senses of the word: 'being absolute' and non 'contaminated' by material gain. In other domains, the enforcement of ritual purity is simultaneously a way (or pretext) to obtain monopolistic control over whole branches of the economic realm and imposing on the public the maintenance of huge parasitic machineries in the interests of whom the Chief Rabbinate (the dispenser of the kashruth certificates) does not hesitate, at least in some cases, to appear quite undisguised as a blackmailer body.

Notwithstanding the unequivocal statement of the Supreme Court, that kashruth is only for those who want it, the State and the public institutions *force* kashruth on everyone who is in need of their hospitals, ships, planes, schools, rest homes, on those who are called to serve in the Army and who are incarcerated in prisons; and in face on practically everyone in all walks of life. Issues of kashruth and related matters are subject to controversy, interference and transactions *in the highest echelons* (coalition bargaining, the illegal refusal of the Ministry of Industry to grant import licenses for non-kosher food, etc.; on the *municipal level* (e.g. the fight of the Jerusalem Religious Council against the closing of unhygienic abattoirs and also on the *private level* (e.g. the libel proceedings brought by a Jerusalem non-kosher butcher shop against Orthodox distributors of leaflets accusing it of selling carrion).

The affairs of *Shalom* and *Marbek* (when the former, because of the Cabinet crisis it involved, received international publicity) may serve to illustrate the *pure* and *impure* forms of fanaticism of the Chief Rabbinate:

In the case of 'Shalom', the Rabbinate threatened not only to refuse to grant a kashruth certificate to Israel's largest passenger vessel if it implements its project to have, in addition to a kosher kitchen, a non-kosher one with a non-kosher dining room, but to withdraw such a certificate from all ships in the ZIM Company, and in addition, when such a certificate was granted by American rabbis - to call upon American Jewry to boycott all Israeli ships. This case, where material gain was insignificant, is an example of pure fanaticism, since the main aim was to prevent passengers, principally Jews, from deciding freely which kitchen they preferred. After the capitulation by the government, the socialist trade union paper, 'Davar' stated that the time was not yet ripe to grant Israeli Jews this right.

Contrary to this is the case of 'Marbek': when the opening of this large, modern, hygienic and strictly kosher slaughterhouse (belonging partly to Orthodox kibbutzim) endangered the income of employees from small and unhygienic slaughterhouses around the country, the Chief Rabbinate refused to grant it kashruth certificates. This is a striking example of very impure fanaticism, having nothing to do with ritual purity. An example of perhaps even greater impurity was related in the Knesset by the former State Attorney, G. Hausner. When an examination of sausages labelled as kosher revealed pork content, the Rabbinate, on being informed about it, stated that it was surely by mistake, and asked that the file against the dealer be closed.

It was almost impossible to gather any accurate data (except in one case) concerning the expenses entailed in the employment of the kashruth inspectors in the various hotels, their number and work arrangement. The only informant who spoke without hesitation, the director of a rest house, told me his inspector (who is a full-time employee there) costs him, including his food, about IL 1000 a month (the expenses for his total personnel amount to IL 20,000). 'He is a nice, liberal guy; he doesn't make much trouble. His chief occupations are playing cards and making children.'

Furthermore, I discovered the following:
a. hotels who pledge to keep only a kosher kitchen, supervised by the Chief Rabbinate, can obtain a government development loan; thus even the largest ones (e.g. Hilton) accept this condition;

b. most hotels pay the kashruth inspectors *more* than they are asked to, in order to make them work *less* - any less zeal on their part can improve the food and save a lot of money;
c. Government Tourist Office guides are formally forbidden to direct buses in Jewish localities to non-kosher hotels and restaurants.

All my efforts to obtain the exact number of kashruth inspectors employed, and data about their incomes, were fruitless. According to the Ministry of Religious Affairs, there are only a few hundred of them. Members of the Knesset from left wing parties speak about thousands (four or more). Taking into consideration the number of hotels, restaurants, hospitals, army camps, factories ships, etc., the latter figure seems to be the more probable one.

SHABBES! SHABBES!

Two episodes characteristic of Sabbath in Israel:

A big private car stops at the gasoline station near Caesarea, and while the attendant fills it up a young man approaches the passengers, asking them to sign a petition of the 'League Against Religious Coercion' for a 'Sabbath without chains'. His request seems reasonable indeed - those driving on the Sabbath are certainly opponents of the curtailment of freedom by religious coercion. But nonetheless, where religion is concerned, neither reason nor coherence govern Israeli public life or the attitudes of the population. Although three of the passengers signed without hesitation, the other three (members of Herut) refused: 'What impertinence, to come with such a petition! We are a Jewish State, aren't we - and not a nation like all the others. The government is certainly right in safeguarding the sanctity of the Sabbath.'

The deep national indignation (extreme, if one can judge from party allegiance) prevents these citizens from realising the contradiction between their assertion and the fact of their travelling on the Sabbath. And probably, they did not think what their attitude would have been if they did not own a private car, but, in order to get to the beach, had to queue (sometimes an hour or more) in the boiling July sun, awaiting a *Sherut*, which, incidentally, a poor man with many children could not afford.

The thousands of cars which pass Caesarea in search of less-crowded bathing areas seem to be a de facto referendum against the enforcement of Orthodox traditions on the population. But, it is rather doubtful if a sizable number of those passengers would display a less incoherent attitude (or apathy concerning the liberties of the individual) than the passengers of the big black Lark. Otherwise it would be unthinkable that medieval features should characterize the Israeli Sabbath.

In contrast to the non-religious public, the Orthodox are anything but indifferent. They carry out their offensive using various tactics: sometimes by shrewd and slow progress; in other cases, through political blackmail, and in some places, it often takes the form of undisguised physical assault. In these latter cases, the protection the police provide to the attacked citizen is rather inefficient. The attackers are usually not even arrested, or are punished with a small penalty.

Similar to this incoherency is the situation in which a driver who approaches an unknown locality on the eve of the Sabbath is uncertain whether or not he can fill up his tank there. And woe to the driver who has engine trouble. Except in the Arab localities, no garages are open, and if the breakdown does not occur on the Haifa-Tel Aviv-Jerusalem highway where patrol cars of the Auto Club operate, he will have to abandon his car, and return on Sunday to take it for repairs. Haifa, the most liberal of all the towns from the point of view of religion is a model of contradictions: while bus transportation is almost regular, the laws of the Sabbath are rigorously safeguarded under the earth and on the sea. The great port of the country is paralyzed (in violation of international conventions), cargo ships are, with few exceptions, not permitted to unload (which costs the State enormous sums) and if a ship with immigrants arrives late on a Friday afternoon, the immigrants nearly always have to wait in front of the closed gates of the Promised Land for about 36 hours.

The underground railway is also paralyzed. When planned, its budget was calculated on an increased income on the Sabbath, but due to a pressure by Mapai ministers on the local leaders, the decision was reversed, and for years the undergrounds have been running with a serious deficit.

On Yom Kippur, the broadcasting service is also paralyzed and in a country practically in a state of war, the population is cut off from local sources of information from what could be emergency orders for 30 hours!

At Lydda Airport, foreign planes arrive and depart on the Sabbath, but not those of El Al, and it is completely closed on Yom Kippur. The post office works irregularly, depending on the momentary situation in the government coalition, and the threat of foreign airlines to curtail their services if telegraph services at least do not function. Israeli civil aviation (El Al) is one of the sore points of the Orthodox, causing friction, due to a wide range of demands, such as closing the airport to all traffic on the Sabbath, to closing at least its restaurant (by threatening withdrawal of the kashruth certificate) and the request that every plane should have its own kashruth inspector... paid, of course, by the company.

Part of the Sabbath observance enforcement is regulated by law; a greater part by municipal by-laws, and a still larger part by an ever-worsening 'status quo' regulated, as mentioned before, secret agreements and internal instructions. So, for example, until a few years ago, on holidays lasting more than one day fresh milk was distributed, but this arrangement was cancelled in many places because of the veto of local religious councils.

The Orthodox had no choice but to accept the fact that in some of the enterprises *has* to be done on Sabbath lest the whole service break down. This is done through special permits from the Ministry of Work (harassed by incessant interference of rabbis and religious councils) or by a special Inter-Ministerial Committee also including the Prime Minister and the Minister of Religious Affairs, the latter aiming to reduce the work to a minimum and have it done by non-Jewish workers.

Illustrative is the example of coincidence and conflict of religious and nationalistic prejudices which greatly complicated the operation of the paper mill in Hadera. Since sacred literature is also printed on the product of this single paper mill in the country, the Chief Rabbinate threatened to boycott it, if the 'atmosphere' of the enterprise was not in accordance with Orthodox prescripts. First, kashruth in workers' kitchen has to be strictly observed (it is superfluous to mention that the inspector is paid by the enterprise) and since there is absolutely no possibility of closing on the Sabbath, the work has to be done by non-Jews. The maintenance of machinery is supervised by Arab workers from the neighboring villages. However, here the complication started.

Attendance of machines is skilled work, and no skilled worker will agree to work only once a week. So it was necessary to engage these workers throughout the week. This was strongly opposed by the Jewish workers, reared on chauvinistic propaganda, and they turned to their trade union (this occurred at a time when work was scarce): 'Throughout all the years, we have been told that the Arabs are enemies of the State and that it is better to have no contact with them. Now they are engaged as skilled workers, while we Jews have to wait a long time until we attain the same status.' I was informed that the 'ideal' solution suggested by the Histadrut and accepted by the paper mill was: The Arab workers work part of their time as skilled workers (on the

Sabbath, of course) and part of the time they do unskilled work. How much does the solution of the combined forms of prejudice raises the price of the product I was unable to ascertain. But it is certain that the price is paid by the consumer.

While speaking about paper, it should be noted that Israel is perhaps the only country in the world where no newspaper appears on the weekly day of rest. And, still concerning paper (and pencil), the author had the following experience a short time ago: He asked the directress of a hostel for academic immigrants to arrange a meeting for him with the residents in order to discuss immigration problems and ask them to fill out a questionnaire. He suggested one Friday evening, since on that evening most of the tenants are at home. The request was turned down, since the premises belong to the Jewish Agency, she could not give permission for public writing to take place there on a Friday evening. In the same vein: the author was invited to deliver a lecture in the House of Culture in Herzliya on a Friday evening, the director found it most natural that I should arrive in my *private* car, but I was forbidden to smoke in the *Municipal* Hall.

It was mentioned previously that almost nowhere are cinema performances held on Friday evening, and theatre performances are held in only a few places. (The Ministry of Education gives a subsidy only to those travelling theatrical ensembles who agree not to play on Friday evening, but it accepts without hesitation antedated or postdated receipts). Museums are closed on the Sabbath until the evening (while working-class people throughout the world visit them exactly on that day of rest). However, paradoxes are not lacking: nightclubs are open on Friday evenings (paying a small fine for the violation of the by-laws) so you can see a striptease but cannot enjoy Molière, a soccer game or a musical matinee on the Sabbath.

There were a few attempts by progressive actors and stage directors to arrange 'private' theatrical performances in Tel Aviv on Friday evenings, and there was an enthusiastic response from the public, but these performances were thwarted by the local authorities.

PURE AND IMPURE FANATICISM IN THE CEMETERY [2]

Similar to the issues of kashruth, matters connected with the dead also have two aspects: of pure fanaticism (compliance with primitive beliefs

2. The quotations in this paragraph are from three articles by A. Nesher on burial in Israel ('Ha'aretz', 19, 21, 23/65)

and rituals, not connected with pecuniary gain) and of impure fanaticism - where the impurity stems not from the uncleanliness of the dead, but from the greediness of those who hold the monopoly over burials and cemeteries.

An example of pure (and perhaps the most shocking) fanaticism is the case of the child who died in Pardess Hanna and whose body remained unburied for several days because burial in the local cemetery was forbidden by the rabbi because of the child's non-Jewish mother. Another example, is the macabre-grotesque case of the door of the chamber of the deceased in Hadassah Hospital in Jerusalem. This hospital, perhaps the most modern in the Middle East, has a very serious 'constitutional deficiency' - its chamber for the deceased is directly linked to the rest of the building. Therefore, all the cohanim hospitalized in this leading Medical Center are in danger of becoming impure by 'contact' with the dead, which is strictly forbidden to them (according to ancient taboos), lest the dead contaminate them with their impurity. Under pressure from the Chief Rabbinate and the American Orthodoxy, the hospital was forced to build a second iron door which automatically closes when the first one is opened, and by this 'separation' the purity of the hospitalized cohanim is ensured. The complicated mechanism breaks down from time to time... and then, after a few days, one can read protests of the Rabbinate concerning the unbearable state of affairs in the hospital. Also, according to the original plans, the dead had to be transported to the chamber of the deceased through underground corridors, but it became known that this arrangement contradicts halachic law, so the deceased now 'descend' (are more or less thrown) from a considerable height - a procedure which is in accordance with religious law, even if it reminds one of blatant contempt for the dead.

Apartheid after death is not limited to the isolation of Jewish dead from those of problematic and non-Jewish origin, but it involves other 'religious', community and class segregation, according to various degrees of piety, economic status, etc., where the privileged ones may be buried (for, say, IL 1,100) in a more respectable plot or even in a cemetery considered full for the simple citizen.

Here, one encounters the impure forms of religious fanaticism. The de facto (though not de jure) monopolistic position of the chevroth kadisha (religious burial societies), governed by their own *Gabbaim* (mainly NRP activists whose activities are practically uncontrolled) allows the extraction of money from the relatives of the deceased.

Since 1965, when the Social Security decided to cover burial expenses by granting a fixed sum to the Chevra Kadisha for each burial, part of the painful and unaesthetic business transaction, such as haggling over burial prices, has stopped.

While this is a step in the proper direction, this Social Security arrangement did not ensure either order or cleanliness in the cemeteries or the abolishment of the illegal practice of extracting money from relatives for the erection of a tombstone. (Illegal, since in most cases the land of the cemeteries is municipal property and does not belong to the chevra kadisha).

'Competition between burial societies sometimes results in unpleasant incidents. It has occurred that, in order to save transportation expenses, those working on 'soil preparation', walked on neighbouring the graves. They have quarrelled over boundaries of burial grounds and stole graves from each other. A major scandal occurred when a competing burial society buried a stranger in a family plot which was already partly occupied. Since the law prohibits the removal of the deceased from his grave, the rabbis could not find any solution to remedy the situation. Cases of grave-seizing and burials in sections belonging to others also occurred in chevroth kadisha of the Oriental communities in Haifa, as disclosed in lawsuits before the Rabbinical Court. One (society) dug a grave and another came in the evening and buried its dead there. It has even happened in Jerusalem that due to the competition, graves were not dug deep enough, and the jackals came and dug there with their snouts'.

Concerning the affair of payments for the license to erect tombstones, A. Nesher writes the following:

'The amount to be paid for the 'tombstone permit' has not been regulated by law. In the State Comptrollers Report, No. 12 of 1962, it is clearly stated: There is no proper and obligatory arrangement concerning the fees which the burial societies are entitled to request and collect for erecting tombstones or buying burial lots during a lifetime. Burial societies continue to collect payments according to their own estimate. 'How much do you collect as fees for tombstone permits?' To this question, a recurrent answer from representatives of burial societies is: 'The poor are buried gratis' or 'From social cases we do not take anything'. Only after investigation did I become wise to the fact that the Jerusalem Sephardic burial society takes 400 IL and perhaps more, from a person of medium income, 'but from the rich takes more, IL 1,000 or more'. Since these societies refuse to open their accounting books, it is difficult to verify these things. But the knowledgeable assured me that the burial societies usually 'make a fortune'.'

One should mention here the fact that burial societies (as well as some of the zealot organizations) have excellent information services. The informants provide them most accurate data, not only about the financial situation of the deceased and his relatives, but also of their business associates, from whom money may be borrowed by the family. A short time ago, another journalist of 'Ha'arez' presented herself at the office of one chevra kadisha, posing as a relative of a dead American Jew whom the family wanted to bury in Israeli soil. She did not receive a definite response concerning the price, since this would be fixed only after American representatives of the 'enterprise' furnished exact details about the financial situation of the deceased.

RELIGIOUS TERRORISM AND UNLAWFUL ACTS OF THE AUTHORITIES

Religious terrorism and oppression encompasses, in different forms and degrees, a wide range of phenomena: from physical attack and rioting, where one deals with terrorism in the narrow and proper sense of the word, to various illegal and discriminatory measures of governmental and public authorities, to more 'customary' political pressures.

As to the activities of the rabbis, it is sometimes difficult to decide which of their acts is illegal or not, in the light of the archaic laws which govern their decisions. That some of their activities were clearly illegal was proven by competent state courts. Equally questionable is the legality of some of the imposed religious practices in the Army.

Holiday-makers travelling by car frequently encounter rioting and almost every Yom Kippur serious injuries are inflicted upon drivers.

There are also incidents of violence against sellers of *Pitta* on Passover, attacks on non-kosher butcher shops, mob violence in connection with autopsies (nearly always incited by Chevra Kadisha functionaries), shouts of 'whore' at 'immodestly' dressed female visitors in some religious quarters, and, very occasionally, the burning of Christian sacred books or unruly behavior on church-owned premises. These last incidents, although rare, generally receive wide coverage in the foreign press, since they usually involve property of a foreign state. Less publicity is given (due to the more local character), to attacks on preachers of Messianic Judaism, such as occurred some years ago in Haifa and Ashdod.

The activists of religious terrorism are mostly Ashkenazi students of yeshivoth or graduates of these schools. This, of course, does not mean that pupils of all the yeshivoth are incited to such violent behavior. However, for these young men (and also the older Orthodox citizen who responds to the call of rabbis to participate in demonstrations) who do participate in rioting and violence, the 'saving of souls' or the 'safeguarding of the sanctity of the Sabbath' is a sacred duty, 'since "all Israelis are responsible for each other" - and they do it without compunction.'

In cases of attack on missionary premises the public at large, although not condoning the act, do not condemn them unequivocally, because of the above-mentioned over-sensitivity in this respect.

While there is no doubt as to the role in xenophobic agitation and occasional acts of violence by students of some yeshivoth and fanatical organizations such as 'The group of activists of the Torah Camp', 'The Guardians of family purity', 'Guardians of the Sabbath', 'The Fund for our children', etc., it is less clear, or at least more difficult to prove the relationship between these bodies and official circles. For example, the Ministry of Religious Affairs and different municipal religious councils, although financial aid from these circles to the anti-missionary bodies is openly admitted.

The question whether the gangs of the Guardians of the Sabbath receive 'only' benefits from some of the religious councils or regular salaries was the subject of an inquiry by the State Comptroller. Ben Haim, the journalist of 'Maariv', began publishing material which disclosed that some of the officials of the Ministry of Religious Affairs were activists of the zealots' fighting organizations. The continuation of the publication of this material was suppressed, due to Orthodox pressure, while the Ministry saw fit to remove its 'Department for Special Activities' from its central premises.

Concerning the non-legal forms of religious coercion by official and semi-official bodies, it will certainly not be an exaggeration to state that religious pressure is more the rule than the exception in nearly all the institutions controlled by the Orthodox parties.

Municipal by-laws enforcing religious observance, which were declared to be illegal by the State courts, have already been mentioned. The spectrum of such prohibitions is a wide one. In a section of Tel Aviv, for example, there is a poster informing the public that taking photographs on the Sabbath is prohibited by the Municipality - the order is disregarded. But in Bnei Brak (one of the centers of religious life and terrorism) the poster at the entrance to its main street indicates that driving there on the Sabbath and on holidays is forbidden by the Municipality; and the driver who disregards this will probably be attacked by religious fanatics. Answering a parliamentary investigation the Minister of Police gave an evasive answer, and it was clear that nothing would be done about this illegal misuse of authority (since the law clearly states that all streets are common property and have to be open to traffic); the best you can expect is that a police patrol car will come to rescue the attacked driver. The fact that, on another poster, an order of the Chief of Staff also forbids Army cars to enter on the Sabbath and holidays only enhances the de facto 'legality' of this illegal order. In order to ensure its fulfilment more efficiently, some of the streets are closed by chains and obstacles. A 'Sabbath chain' on Mount Zion caused the death of sculptor D. Palombo while driving his scooter.

It is obvious that the Chief Rabbinate and the Ministry of Religious Affairs are the center of legal as well as illegal religious coercion. A random sample of incidents will illustrate this: a list of all couples of mixed marriages and their scions was secretly circulated by this Ministry to the local rabbinates, to prevent possible 'infiltration' by marriage of a 'non kosher Jew' into the sacred flock. Repeated refusal to register marriages between a cohen and a divorcee, although legally binding if it once took place, and in at least one case, an attempt to force the husband to divorce his wife, the mother of his child. Rabbinical judgments threatening the cessation of alimony to a woman because her bathing suit (similar to that of thousands of others) was not 'modest' enough while bathing in a mixed pool; or invalidating the right of a mother to bring up her child if she does not light candles on Friday evening [3]; pressure on hotels and other establishments and extraction of money in connection with kashruth certificates, etc., etc.

Among the governmental offices, it is the Ministry of Interior, which by its very nature, can exert maximum illegal pressure, while the Ministry of Social Affairs and the Ministry of Health have a more restricted field of interference.

Some of the activities of the Ministry of Interior in the sphere of influence have already been mentioned. Here we shall only enumerate without comment - the practice of registering (against the will of the person) as non-Jews all those whose mother is not Jewish and sometimes also attempts to withdraw Israeli citizenship in such cases, and even more sordid, in some cases of non-Jewish widows (after the death of their Jewish husband). Another line of 'subtle' pressure is exerted on municipalities: their proposed budget will not be so easily approved if they are not 'generous enough' with the local religious council. The Ministry successfully intervened at the Head Office of Kol Israel and cancelled the

---

3. Cf. Sh. Aloni: 'The Rights of the Child in the State of Israel' and also her articles concerning illegal religious coercion: 'The Rabbi incites the husband to abandon his wife' (Davar' 10.8.65) and 'Mikveh is not a prior condition of marriage' (Davar' 28.7.65).

very popular programme of Sh. Aloni 'Outside Office Hours' because of her disclosures of illegal practices against Reform Jews. Another case in which one of the minor clerks in this office snatched out of a woman's hands her identity card, on which her legally-approved change of name was registered, and 'cancelled' the change on the spot and at his own discretion, since it could result in a rabbi's wrongly approving her marriage to a cohen, etc., etc.

The Ministry of Social Affairs has a more limited field of action although still important, from the point of view of political and religious pressure: illegal distribution of money to religious party activists and exerting pressure by its (social and other) workers on parents to register their children at religious schools, to remove them from non-Jewish boarding schools; even trying to persuade Courts that the parents are unfit to take proper decision, etc. (Many examples can be found in Sh. Aloni's cited book).

Even more restricted are the possibilities of the Ministry of Health, temporarily held by the Orthodox. It is limited to the appointment of a maximum number of party members to administrative posts in hospitals and the appointment (in addition to the regular kashruth-inspectors) of 'religious counsellors', and sometimes to administrative obstruction of post-mortem examination.

Enforcement of Orthodox religious precepts in the Army concerning kashruth and partially also Sabbath observance is supervised by 'Sergeants of Religion' in the units. Chief Army Chaplain Colonel Goren is one of the most powerful and influential figures in Israeli Orthodoxy, and he succeeds in progressively augmenting the influence of the Army Rabbinate. Characteristic of the prevailing spirit of discriminatory practices is the case of a Reform Rabbi, a captain, whose request to be transferred to the Army Rabbinate was turned down, while some almost illiterate Orthodox youngsters easily find places there.

Marked inconsistency is revealed in the enrolment practices of sons of non-Jewish mothers, and also in the exemption of girls, either on grounds of conscientious objection or religious-conscientious objection, from sectarian movements.

In some cases, no patriotic fervor suffices to open the gates of the army camps to boys, some of whom even ignored the fact that their mothers are of Christian origin, while in other cases, similar half-Jews protest that 'If I cannot be buried in a Jewish cemetery, I have no obligation to serve in the Army' and refuse to serve - and are prosecuted. In one such case, the State Attorney's Office intervened in the prosecution recognising that someone who is discriminated against on religious grounds cannot be expected to prove willing to serve in the Army.

While exemption is automatically granted to a girl upon a declaration that she is religious and the presentation of a certificate from the rabbi, it is generally turned down - despite the letter of the law - if the request is solely on conscientious grounds. In one such case, a girl who had been refused exemption on conscientious grounds obtained without difficulty a certificate stating that she was religious. A public scandal ensued when the girl, not wishing to take the easy way out, revealed what had happened.

II. The question which arises quite naturally of why the resistance of the secularist majority against religious oppression is so feeble, unorganized and inefficient requires an intensive and extensive analysis. In this context, only a few remarks will be made, complementing those made in the first paragraph.

Important, in this respect, is the analysis of those forces which are usually in the forefront of the fight against obscurantism: left-wing parties, the intelligentsia, and the rising generation.

Although verbal anti-clericalism appears on their programmes, the struggle for a secular republic does not feature prominently in the practical aims of the left-wing parties. Anti-traditionalist attitudes are even repressed for patriotic reasons.

The fact that religious coercion in the kibbutzim is less oppressive also contributes to the general torpor, since the leaders of the leftist parties are mostly kibbutz veterans. So, except for a few parliamentary skirmishes, no serious attempts were made to withstand religious coercion, and even less to engage in a counter-offensive to free the country altogether from its legal and illegal manifestations.

Another phenomenon of Israeli public life should be mentioned here, a corollary of the coalitionary morals mentioned in the first chapter, referred to by some writers (Prof. Talmon, U. Avnery) as the 'rule of the feudalists'. This expression is inaccurate, as it may be in the proper sociological sense a psychologically revealing one. It expresses the ideology and ethics of politicians (party, trade union, bosses, etc.) which are equally characteristic of the religious and secular ones, that they are if not ex Deo gratia, so by the 'rules of the game', absolute rulers over their fief. They feel that fair play obliges them to honor promises made to the other 'feudalists' (i.e., party representatives) with whom they concluded open or secret agreements but on the other hand, it is absolutely 'honest' to deceive the electorate. Promises made to the public are not binding.

All this necessarily contributes to the depolitization of the masses. Political alienation, feelings of powerlessness against party-machinery and meaninglessness of any political action become dominant.

Converse to the commitment of religious youth, one can witness a far-reaching depolitization and petty bourgeois careerism in the ranks of secular youth. Among the reasons given is the disappointment with any ideology (which is also symptomatic of a considerable number of world's youths), which co-exists, however, with a bad conscience for not fulfilling the pioneering-kibbutz ideals of the old-timers. Thus, in order to escape feelings of remorse and instead of analysing their situation, they tend to escape into indifference and political apathy.

One should not forget that the basically conservative, although presented as progressive, formal and informal education of the youth knows only *one* freedom - national (more exactly, national-religious) freedom. Neither freedom of conscience nor freedom of the individual are values which are spoken about. The reasons therefore seem to be: a) the martyrdom for the 'sanctification of the Name' is presented as supreme Jewish heroism, i.e., for the freedom to confess his own religion, but by no means freedom *from* religion; b) the period of rationalism and emancipation coincides with the beginning of assimilation (and the personal choice in this matter) which evokes all the hostile reactions which were repeatedly mentioned, and again this great period in the victory of the individual is rather underplayed; c) *personal* freedom contradicts collectivistic idolatry.

Nor is there, up till now, an adequate framework (of movement, party, etc.) to organize the struggle against religious oppression. The 'League Against Religious Coercion' did not succeed in mobilizing the masses (the reasons require, again, a special analysis) and, since part of the religious habits became national folklore, to oppose them requires very much stamina and personal determination.

The role of the long military service can also not be underestimated in the process of depolitisation: a considerable number of university students, many of whom are married, have to earn their living when starting their studies at the age of 21-23. Also, until a short time ago, their organizations were ruled by salaried party functionaries, often only nominally students.

A considerable lack of civil courage, characteristic of the adults, as well as the youth is a further factor. Many reasons are responsible. A few should be noted:

Dogmatic collectivistic education in the youth movements instils a reluctancy in the individual to initiate any non-conformist actions, or even the obligation to act *personally*. Therefore, activities contradicting the accepted customs are very rare (characteristic is the very reluctant attitude of most young couples to undergo 'private marriages', even in Hashomer Hazair kibbutzim, arguing: 'It should be as customary'). Even personal courage and obstinancy to go to court on a matter of principle is a rare exception.

Another reason for the passivity of the population stamps from a group made up of Western (and central) European and American immigrants who oppose religious coercion due to its education and liberal-secular traditions stemming from its country of origin. But, their number is relatively small and many of them are old and have lost the fighting spirit. Some of them are still activists in the fight against religious coercion, but those are mostly isolated individuals and not organized groups.

As to the intelligentsia: there are many intellectuals, but no intelligentsia (in the sense of the French or Russian usage of the term) in Israel. Many of the intellectuals are themselves traditionally-minded (the older generation of teachers and writers) and some of them have still not overcome the remorse for not conforming to the pioneering ideal, manual labor. The intellectuals were on the defensive, because of the near hostile and abusive attitude of the authorities which prevailed until a few years ago. Today, they are predominantly engaged in the professional-utilitarian field.

The dread of the professional unemployment of the thirties still influences their thinking. Also, the fact that a considerable number of them are directly dependent on government or public institutions makes them objectively vulnerable, paralyzing the courage to openly oppose official policy.

Last, but not least: the absence of powerful economic groups whose vested interests would be endangered by religious coercion.

The branches which were almost totally annihilated by religious oppression are few (for instance, the pig breeders), while in others, the ensuing higher prices are (mostly) automatically 'transferred' to the customer. For example, as soon as the Dan bus cooperative was granted a raise in fares to compensate for the losses due to not working on the Sabbath, it lost all interest in supporting the fight for public transport on holidays. The same is true for hotel owners, whose 'cost plus' calculation includes the kashruth inspector, the cinema proprietor who calculates his income on a basis of six and not seven days a week, etc., etc.

On the other hand, for the citizen-consumer, the *visibility* of his increased expenses is blurred, since they are dispersed over many items. Nobody has yet calculated how much the Orthodox interpretation of

Divine Law costs him [4], and how much his income would increase if the ships departed on the Sabbath, the cinemas held performances on Friday evening, and if he were not obliged to pay more for kosher meat and to cover the budget of the Ministry of Religious Affairs.

---

4. It is estimated that kosher increases meat prices between 10-30% and the absence of public transportation on Sabbath raises fares by 30%.

4. The Israeli authoritarian personality*

The peer-group becomes the measure of all things; the individual has few defenses the group cannot batten down.

D. Riesman, 'The Lonely Crowd'

---

* This text is a shortened version of a lecture 'Reflections on the Israeli Authoritarian Personality, its Social Significance and Psychological Evaluation' (Tel Aviv, 1965).

I. Nearly twenty years of intensive and extensive research concerning the authoritarian personality and related areas have demonstrated that the personality traits, as described in the Berkeley studies, are somewhat more characteristic of right authoritarianism than general authoritarianism, and that one finds the authoritarian syndrome across groups, time and geographical boundaries (Barker). It is also evident that there are more and less authoritarian cultures, and that a given socio-cultural pattern, may specifically shape the authoritarian type of that milieu.

If the problem of the authoritarian personality in Israel is raised together with the relationship between the dominant ideological values and the authoritarian ideal - everyday observation may reveal a highly contradictory picture.

On the one hand, if it is true that 'for the authoritarian character there exist, so to speak, two sexes, the powerful one and the powerless one' (Fromm) and 'hence (he) emphasises strength and toughness as supreme value, considers love and sympathy as signs of weakness' (Saenger) and if ethnocentrism, conformism, intolerance and intellectual rigidity are dominant traits of this personality, an unbiased observer will probably be impressed by the obsession of a considerable section of Israeli youth with toughness and 'manhood', its narrow-minded chauvinism (accompanied by a feeling of superiority, especially towards non-Israeli Jews) its (panic) fear of revealing any signs of weakness [1], and its 'segregatory' tendencies [2], all of which are positive diagnostic signs of an authoritarian personality.

On the other hand, it is sufficient to visit a class of many of Israeli schools, where the teacher has a hard time conducting a lesson, or to hear the lamentations of a visiting choreographer (or coach, etc.) about the many weeks it took the members of the team to appear on time for rehearsal; to hear incidents about army life, where the social barrier between privates and officers is probably less marked than in any other existing army, to consider the fact that the *kibbutzim* are perhaps the only really voluntary egalitarian-collectivist settlement movements in the world, where *direct* democracy is practised. Also to observe the general disregard for municipal regulations and bylaws, and to remember that bad manners and boastfulness are cherished traits of the Sabra's self-image; to pause for a second thought and ask oneself if this striking feature is not exactly the absence of authoritarianism but perhaps indicative of an elementary orderliness.

1. 'Envy the Frightened' by Y. Dayan and our observation in the previous chapter.
2. Cf. among others 'No Trespassing' by H. Alon.

The first question of semanticism which arises here is what is the opposite of rigid authoritarian discipline - lack of discipline or reasonable discipline? A second question concerns the identification of authoritarianism with militaristic tendencies and its opposite with tolerance and democracy. This question will be encountered later.

Taking into consideration the traits of ethnocentrism, glorification of strength and the prevailing admiration for the Army - the same unbiased observer will accept as natural the results of studies such as those of Chudnovski (revealing tendencies towards dictatorial ideals on the part of a considerable section of the youth, facts which caused a tremendous public uproar); of Adar and Adler (concerning the education in the spirit of nationalism); those of the author (concerning prejudiced attitudes in various fields). Perhaps less convincing is the idea put forward by Minkovitz and Shaked in their report of a pilot study on the authoritarian personality in Israel: 'In view of the prevailing impression that in our society (and especially in the population of old-timers) democratic, egalitarian and tolerant values are stressed and attitudes favouring progress in economics and inter-class relations are cultivated, we expected that the tendency towards authoritarianism, as measured by the F-Scale, will be less in the Israeli society - and particularly in the intellectual sphere - than in other countries'. [3]

Every author is of course free to depart from any hypothesis which seems to him plausible, and which will be either confirmed or refuted by his research. One should only bear in mind that the hypothesis may influence the technique of research, which again may influence the final results. I shall return to this point later.

Minkovitz and Shaked mention the prevailing impression that begs the question - *where* does it prevail? In our opinion, first, in the official texts and among the old-timers themselves. Contrary to this, one very seldom hears spontaneously that the Israeli society and way of life is democratic (and for the moment I'll abstain from discussing what democracy *really is)* from people who immigrated from countries with a de-

---

3. Cf. Minkovitz-Shaked: 'The Authoritarian Personality' (Megamot, March, 1962). Concerning the supposed democratic attitudes of the old-timers (implying a dissimilar trend in the new immigrants, especially those from the Afro-Asian countries): there is no doubt *some* truth as to the backwardness and conservatism of a sizable segment of those immigrants, but, as we pointed out repeatedly, any generalization may lead to involuntary dangerous prejudices. So, as stated elsewhere, immigrants from 'Oriental' countries are much more tolerant in religious matters as opposed to the fanaticism of the Ashkenazi obscurantists. A recent study by Sh. Eisenberg also does not support the thesis of a greater tolerance of the generation of the 'founding fathers'.

mocratic tradition of respecting the rights of the *individual* and of *tolerance* towards differing opinions and ways of life.

Without the slightest doubt there were almost no barriers of class distinction in the pre-war Israeli (Palestinian) society. The heritage of this egalitarianism is indeed one of the most positive traits of Israeli reality and values (for example in the medical care received by an unskilled labourer in a hospital is the same as that of the senior manager of his enterprise). It is also true that there prevails a very liberal approach to extra-marital sex relations and to abortion... with the highly paradoxical situation of simultaneous extreme intolerance towards mixed marriages. [4]

Apart from this, as was previously suggested, a striking deviation from the classical pattern of the authoritarian personality is the absence of affirmation of discipline (on the contrary) and the absence of the glorification of the father-figure (on the contrary - the father is almost by definition something inferior, 'diasporic'). And though it would be somewhat inaccurate to speak about a total absence of glorification of an individual leader [5], the supreme authority is one's (narrow) collective.

Also, the obsessive traits which are characteristic of the authoritarian personality are not characteristic of its local variation, although one could speak about a mannerism of 'Sabraic simplicity' and institutionalized aggression.

The basic question concerning the Israeli authoritarian personality deals with the degree to which egalitarianism is identical with democracy... if this much used and abused concept also includes tolerance and freedom from prejudice.

In my opinion, democracy *is* egalitarian in the affirmation of the basic equality of humans and their rights, but in no way as an *equality of uniforms,* which is often ruthlessly intolerant towards any deviation from the group norms or non-conformism concerning 'collective ideology' or the 'customs of the gang'.

In this sense the Israeli egalitarianism (in a society where the psycho-

---

4. Many Israeli girls (with marked national consciousness) will not hesitate to have a love affair and sexual relations with a non-Jew, but will categorically refuse to marry him.
5. It is significant that perhaps the most popular figure in the eyes of Israeli youth (even those far from his political conceptions) is General M. Dayan, the commandant during the Sinai Campaign; famous not only as a military leader but also for his mannerless 'Sabraic straightforwardness' and his Blitzkrieg conquest of women. If military virtues are one facet of his personality, unruly and rowdy behaviour in disregarding regulations is the other.

therapist is daily confronted with the 'order': 'I want to be as all are') [6] is an egalitarianism of uniforms with an over-emphasis on conformity and a rigid intolerant characteristic of the most *dissimilar* circles.

Intolerance is equally characteristic of orthodox-religious groups to whom a member of a slightly different religious circle or movement is a traitor, of youth movements to whom those youngsters who decide not to go to 'Nachal' are traitors, for the kibbutz to whom he is a traitor who after long soul-searching reaches the conclusion that he must leave since he will find more happiness outside and definitely in the eyes of the public at large he is an abject traitor who leaves the country. The following examples can only be regarded as an intolerant egalitarianism of uniforms.

In a left wing kibbutz the agenda for a Youth Group included the item: should 16 year-old girls be free to wear pink (and not only white) underwear or is this a sign of bourgeois coquetry. The fact that no such permission was granted is more or less irrelevant since in my humble opinion underwear (and all they cover) should be the exclusive concern of the individual and free from social or public interference.

A severe trauma of a young patient of mine was the educational crusade of his instructor who shamed him for his preference for playing records while alone and not with his peers.

The remark of a ten year-old girl saying to her psychotherapists: but how is it (Elisheva), that such a nice girl as you is living in town? The implication being that anything that is worth something can be found only in the kibbutz. [7]

It is rather difficult to convey adequately the reaction of another girl, a nineteen year-old student, who was horrified to hear that one of our popular actors is a communist.

On the other hand, it *is* possible to reproduce exactly the slogan of

---

6. Equally illustrative for the other-directed attitudes and conformism is the fact, that Israeli students, when given a seminary work, almost automatically ask, with which of the fellow students will they carry it out and the anecdote about the young man, married a few weeks ago, whose only complaint is, that his wife has no pubic hair, and to the remark that this really is not important answers: 'yes, but what will the "gang" say?'

7. M. Weiberger: The Individual and the Community (in 'Man Alone').
A colleague of mine had the following experience with a 15 year-old girl patient (to whom she interpreted her hysterical symptoms as related to her repressed sexual interests), after she returned from a holiday in her kibbutz: 'Now I know that you were entirely wrong with your idea about my illness. This Sabbath we had a discussion in the Youth Group, and it was *decided* that at our age sexual matters should not preoccupy us, *so* you see that you were wrong'.

the Ministry of Education, a symbol of cultural intolerance: 'One tongue instead of seventy languages', or another appearing in the early fifties in hospitals and clinics citing Ben Yehuda: 'Speak Hebrew and you will be healthy'. Fortunately, most new immigrants were unable to read this slogan.

The intolerant opposition to mixed marriages and the Israeli educational curriculum as a source of dogmatic thinking and narrow-minded ethnocentrism, is dealt with in other chapters, so no further explanation is necessary.

If intolerance towards deviation from strict group norms is still relative, in other fields it becomes absolute and totally uninhibited in relation to emigrants who are the worst traitors. While a liberal approach considers such a decision first of all in a personal affair and views it as a failure of the individual to find his place and happiness in the country, the reaction is to despise those who seek the 'pot of flesh'; against those people the most inhuman gestures (eg. asking the Jewish organizations not to help them in the lands of their arrival) as well as illegal actions by governmental authorities are considered as wholly justified. [8]

If in this context I have not mentioned the chauvinism of the extreme right or the dogmatism and fanaticism of all the religious parties, the reason is that it is quite *natural* to find in every society conservative forces which endorse values whose affirmation is predominantly characteristic of the authoritarian personality. However, in Israel, the striking feature is exactly that of egalitarianism of uniforms of would-be democrats: the chauvinistic and parochial educational system which shapes the present day younger generation's outlook was established by socialists (who are also active supporters of the national-religious isolationism). The Liberal (!) Party answering a questionnaire of the 'League Against Religious Coercion' stated bluntly: 'no wrong is done to a Jew if he is married by a rabbi', while an article in the periodical of this same party (Bentov: 'A Scarecrow named the Division of the People', Tmurot, 1963) advocates urgent reform after exposing the sufferings of people as a result of the antihumanistic laws of marriage and divorce. The article concludes that this is to enable Jews to marry Jews since marriage between Jews and Christians is not permitted.

8. This spirit finds adequate expression in the official forms to be filled out if someone wants to renounce their Israeli citizenship. Its text almost reminds one of the excommunication rites and means to provoke deepest guilt-feelings. Some data about this theme can be found in a series of articles 'Why Israel persecutes the emigrants' (Ha'aretz, 1964).

These are strange symptoms of a democratic and tolerant society, and the stubborn refusal to see that this approval of segregation is no better than that of other racial ideologies is a sure indication of an authoritarian personality.

II. Absolute conformity to group norms, as stated before, i.e. unconditional acceptance of the collective authority, is a basic trait of the Israeli authoritarian personality and also a dominant trend of the psychodynamics of a very sizable number of young Israelians... in their flight into the 'lonely crowd'.

Buber's thesis reveals that the admiration of the collective does not stem so much from ideological causes but from the fear of the individual of loneliness and responsibility [9].

This acceptance of the authority of the collective and public opinion is characteristic of the authoritarian personality in more democratic societies as against that in totalitarian regimes, but by no means does it indicate an anti-authoritarian personality structure. 'In more democratic societies, submission to the dictates of the group, blind conformity, takes the place of submission to a strong leader. Such submission occurs at the expense of individual self-expression' (Saenger) [10].

Furthermore, the condescending attitude towards the 'diasporic' parents (a stereotype created by the parents themselves, at least by the East-European 'founding fathers') seems to be as much a source of the glorification (not of the father figure, but of one's peer group) as the fetishism of collectivism itself; as expressed in the 'Poem of the Children of Tnuva' [11]: 'Instead of milk they give us cream/Instead of mother we have a nurse'.

The lack of discipline encouraged by parents and ideologists, who consider lack of inhibitions as a sign of strength and mental stability, is the second marked deviation of the Israeli authoritarian personality from its 'classic' model. [12]

9. Cf. Buber: 'Between Man and Man'. We emphasize in other texts the remarkable discrepancy between heroic readiness to self-sacrifice in military situations and general lack of civil courage. Another aspect of the one-sided collectivistic reflexes is that Sabra's try to avoid competitive situations but if they are forced into such situations they show very little idea of fair play.
10. Cf. Saenger: Social Psychology of Prejudice.
11. 'Tnuva', a large cooperative enterprise, here symbolizes the community ownership and belonging with a flavour of absence of 'personal' parenthood.
12. A rather far-reaching parallellism between the child-centeredness in Israel and the USA can be noted, and also concerning the rigid conformity to groupnorms. This latter was described by E. Duvergny ('USA - essai d'une mythologie

I am convinced that any psychological evaluation which fails to take into consideration these specific aspects can give a valid picture of the Israeli authoritarian personality. For instance, it seems that if the ending of the item 'No sane, normal decent person could ever think of hurting a close friend or relative' would be 'someone of his *gang*' (or *'movement')*, the answers may be different than if one is dealing with the *family* (which is not an object of high esteem, or even a *single* good friend the relationship to whom still implies a person to person relationship). Also the item 'there is hardly anything lower than a person who does not feel a great love, gratitude and respect for his parents' may elicit different responses if its ending would be 'to his community'.

As to the item 'what youth needs most is strict discipline, rugged determination and the will to work and fight for family and country', its composite structure makes the item analysis difficult. In the case of a positive response it is difficult to ascertain whether one associates the devotion to the family with the strength of the attachment to the country, or whether one truly marries both ideas. By changing the ending into 'for community and country' with an additional item in which only family would be mentioned, this point could have been clarified.

One item which seems to us altogether inappropriate in view of the absence of respect for *privacy* in Israel, is: 'Nowadays more and more people are prying into matters that should remain personal and private'. The individual is troubled often enough by bureaucratic machinery as well as by his indiscreet neighbours - so that the affirmation of this item contra-indicates a more liberal and democratic attitude (and indeed it was among the items with the lowest discriminatory power in the above-mentioned study of Sh. Eisenberg and also in the current study of one of my students. In some groups the correlation between total authoritarianism and this item was even negative).

I have no intention of criticising the paper by Minkovitz and Shaked, which the authors themselves consider as a pilot study, and also since the basic question which I have to pose is: to what degree can the original (or shortened) F-scale be considered as an adequate instrument in Israel, a question that can of course be asked concerning the 'transfer' of almost any test from one culture to another. My critical remarks relate exclusively to this general problem.

I have the impression that if the authors' point of departure was not that of the 'official' credo, namely that Israel is a democratic and tole-

américaine') as the most intolerant model of democracy (i.e. the tyranny of public opinion).

rant society, they would have probably been forced into an analysis of the specific features of the 'egalitarianism of uniforms' and of the dogmatic acceptance of the authority of the group. This again suggests:
a. it is appropriate to change some of the items in the way indicated above and
b. some questions related to sex and social life (especially in those fields where there exists legal encroachment on civil liberties) could furnish highly revealing data.

One could of course object to this on the basis that the construction plan of the F-scale (in contrast to the E and A-S scales) is such as to manifestly avoid ideological problems. However, as the authors themselves state, there are some questions with such a flavour; and, also, at least some items which can be formulated so that the ideological content becomes less manifest.

For instance the following statements seem to us appropriate:
— One feels the greatest pride while watching the brave Israeli boys on their tanks and the girl-soldiers with their sten-guns at an Independence Day Parade.
— Military service has a high educational value in shaping the character of the man and it should not be abolished even if it is not required for security reasons. (Toughness, chauvinism)
— No responsible government should permit missionaries to propagate unhindered their religion, thus causing some people to become alienated from their nation and the faith of their fathers. (Anti-democratic religious-nationalist practices)
— There is no resemblance between the Israeli laws preventing mixed marriage in order to preserve the purity of the Jewish people and the racial laws of the fascist countries. (Isolation of belief and disbelief systems)
— Marching in the Parade on the First of May, following the leaders of the Movement and carrying flags and banners one feels that the supreme goal of the individual is to merge into his collective.
— There can be no interest of such importance to any individual that it should not be subordinated to the interests of the community.
— The great contribution of Socialism is the recognition of the sanctity of work itself, and not for the material goods it produces.
— The collective educational system in the kibbutz is a basis for the formation of a new superior type of man for whom the community and not personal or familial egotism is the supreme object of his strivings and loyalties. (Secular surrogates of religion)

Various phenomena of Israeli social life and ideals (especially in the kibbutzim and the youth movements) suggest that one deals here with predominantly 'left-authoritarianism' and the last-mentioned items are intended to gauge this tendency. However, one could object to some studies of Rokeach and others which found that subjects high in left-authoritarianism were at the same time low in ethnocentrism, which is certainly not the case in Israel. True, those studies were *not* carried out in socialist countries, in which chauvinism is today a quite outstanding trait in the public at large, and it is highly probable that the authoritarian personalities of those countries would themselves reveal a marked degree of ethnocentricity. The important question, of course, is, what *is* right and what *is* left in any particular socialist country.

III. The constant preoccupation of Israeli youth with physical strength and courage and some caricaturistic demonstrations of toughness and '(he)manhood' (lack of inhibitions, loud speech, the ideal of the parachutist, about whom, all the women are 'crazy', overemphasis of masculine symbols (in a style which is a curious mixture of Biblical and Hollywood-type motives; see the 'Exodus') are dominant traits of the Israeli authoritarian personality.

Examples from literary documents can testify to this, as well as the derogatory expression: 'this too is a man' (if someone drives carefully or was not in prison during army service), the continuous opposition to the abolishment of the 'discipline of water' (i.e. rationed water supply on long marches in youth movements) despite scientific proof that it is totally useless as training since one cannot adapt to lack of water, and the hypertrophy of signs of 'masculinity' (characteristic for boys *and* girls) illustrated equally well by the expression of supreme praise in military slang: 'a girl with balls', and, on the other hand, by the shameful acknowledgment of a 17 year old girl, that she *knows* how to cook, since this evidently contradicts the idealized model: '...for who has not seen the archetypical Israeli girl, rifle in hand, on innumerable book jackets, posters and advertisements? Even Israeli girls trying to make Hollywood by posing in the nude are photographed with a sten gun' [13].

My encounters with this obsession of masculinity are among the most peculiar episodes of my psychotherapeutic work... and constitute some of my outright failures.

For example, the encounter with the 18 year old youngster who came (later it became clear, that he was not satisfied with his previous psy-

---

13. In 'Commentary', 1960, January.

chotherapist) with the urgent 'order' to 'make a man' of him (so that he will be as all others are). During the anamnesis, to my question about his mother's state of health, he answered: 'not so well, she has headaches and is feeble... and altogether she is... not a man'. When I remarked that she may indeed have some reasons for that, he answered impatiently: 'You do not understand this.' His answer was the same concerning his sister, whom he did not hold in high esteem - she was also not a man. (I was sorry indeed not to be able to fulfil his order and make a man of him).

More serious was the case of another young man, who, after the death of his father became the only provider of his family and who quitted his job as a waiter, because of the ridicule of his friends: 'this too is a *man's job*'.

In another case, it was revealed in the analysis that his way of life, his choice of profession, marriage, divorce, etc., were conditioned by his idealism of boastfulness and showmanship, and after I had pointed out to him that all this was superfluous, since it goes against his warm and human nature, he said pathetically: 'Yes, doctor, but what will then remain?' To my request to draw a sketch of the 'real man' as perceived by the 'gang', he wrote the following lines:

'His outward appearance: tall, broad shoulders and narrow hips, his arm muscles are bulging and his face is beautiful and masculine at the same time. On his lips there is a slight despising smile, his walk is agile and he is full of self-confidence, which raises him above his surroundings.

His qualities demonstrated courage, security in his actions and his speech, brilliant in his cleverness and sharp tongue. In no situation, be it the most disconcerting or difficult, does he lose his coolness or poise. Without the least effort he conquers the hearts of the opposite sex, and he is able to renounce any woman as if she were unworthy of him.

In the memory of the forsaken (woman) there will always remain a feeling that there never was and never will be anyone like him. He can dominate his friends as their leader and idol, without any apparent effort, as if it comes to him automatically.

In short, perfection from all points of view, without failures or weakness, maximum efficiency and cleverness; in summary: a beautiful, pleasant and refined machine.' [14]

14. A much more distressing aspect of this glorified 'masculinity' is revealed in the case of Meir Har Zion, one of those legendary figures found in the war and post-war annals of almost every country, whose heroic deeds as a semi-guerrilla fighter made him the idol of every commando-fighter, and whose record of lawless practices later made him a danger to society.

'What do you feel when you stick a knife in the back of the enemy?' Meir puts down his half eaten bread, looks ahead with cold, blue and somewhat watery

Some remarks concerning friendship ('companionship') and sex, as the Israeli authoritarian personality sees them, and the mores in this field, are appropriate here.

As to sex, Saenger (op. cit.) states: 'While sex is important to the authoritarian person, it is experienced as overpowering or submitting, and is not associated with affection.' Generally speaking the realm ('atmosphere') of friendship and eroticism is characterized by a curious oscillation between 'companionship', in a 'going steady' and rather Victorian style, with many more 'monogamic' obligations than rights and between predominantly unemotional sexual relations. In overemphasising the absence of sentimentality one can discern the semi-ascetic attitude of the *fighter*, who is wholly dedicated to the great ideal and who feels that any emotional involvement with a woman is detrimental to his devotion to the ideal [15].

It seems that there is a direct relationship between this ideal and the fact that perhaps the most frequent complaint in marital crises is the complaint of the wife about the lack of tenderness on the part of her husband. True, I never conducted a Kinsey-style study (and do not hold a very high opinion about such surveys) but in hundreds of cases of counseling and therapy, I have had the opportunity to hear about the most intimate aspects of marital life and I was shocked by the fact that the number of couples who exchanged endearing words during intercourse was almost nil.

Does this mean that the man considers his partner as a mere object for his gratification? Definitely not: in most cases the man feels a clear obligation to satisfy his partner. He considers the *ejaculatio retardata* (which is considered a sign of masculinity to be proud of) the most appropriate way of achieving this, according to the equation: the longer the act lasts the more chance the woman has of experiencing orgasm. This half-truth expresses a purely mechanical-physiological conception of the sexual experience, disregarding the possibility that it may also be even more important for the woman to feel a physiological gratification. (This is not intended to mean that one does not find girls who also sub-

---

eyes, and answers in a guttural voice: 'It is a supreme feeling, the most marvellous feeling. You feel that you are a man'. ('Ha'aretz', 7 December, 1965)
15. This is certainly not an Israeli characteristic. If Nimrod, cited in the previous chapter fits this picture, the same is true for revolutionaries such as Pavle Vlasov in Gorki's: 'The Mother' or Mitja in Davico's 'The Poem'. (One should especially note the episodes where they are 'training' toughness toward the beloved woman as preparation for the task of the unconditional revolutionary).

scribe to the ideology that the sexual act has to be 'simple and without unnecessary complication'). I would think that appropriate items in the F-scale, such as 'No real man will allow his feeling towards a woman to deter him from his task or goal', may reveal some important attitudes in this field.

IV. The social role of the Israeli authoritarian personality reveals itself especially in the following three domains: education, the specific public atmosphere which may also characterize the interpersonal relationships, and in the political field, the rule of the 'local bosses' (usually mayors of small towns or secretaries of Trade Unions) who govern their 'fief' with an iron hand and sometimes ruthless disregard for the law, with the knowledge that they have the full support of their party.

The specific feature of the local authoritarian personality, namely the cult of toughness but without respect for law and order reflecting the sacred formula of the 'desert generation' (with adequate 'desert' manners of mannerlessness) gives the Israeli society its folkloristic atmosphere of Wild West or more precisely 'Wild East'. This element of the Wild East in social relations was especially marked in the fifties, parallel with the transformation of the Yishuv from a solidary minority into a heterogeneous majority. Simultaneously, one witnessed a gradual disappearance of the former stabilizing factors (the authority of the collective, and of the egalitarianism of uniforms; thus a certain disintegration of the pattern occurs) when public life became characterized in its individual and collective plans by an uninhibited competition using legal and semi-legal means, which reminds one of the period of early capitalism in the West.

To what extent this contempt of legality has a 'traditional' background, stemming from Mandatory times, when the laws were those of a foreign and perhaps adversary power and the only authority towards whom moral obligation was felt was that of the national movements, cannot be explicitly explained.

The influence of the specific aspect of the Israeli authoritarian personality is felt, as stated, first of all in the field of education, i.e. the extreme tolerance towards the phenomena of aggression and rudeness in children.

When Israeli parents watch with indifference and even concealed pride how their children, growing up in the streets, seem to be moved by a conditioned reflex to pick up a stone and throw it at their playmates ('Oh, what darlings are our free sons') and when the educational authorities forbid even elementary disciplinary measures against wild and disorderly behaviour, one can only speak of an institutionalized anomaly in line with the national mythology of the 'uninhibited youth' who should not be restrained in his emotional outlet, who is less responsible to teachers or parents and more to his peer group or the instructor of Gadna or his youth movement.

I repeat, it is an anomalistic phenomenon since the cult of the 'uninhibited he-man' very easily becomes the prologue to waywardness and the first step towards delinquency - a fact which the creators of the national mythology stubbornly refuse to admit.

Some years ago, during his visit to Israel, Justice S. Leibovitz predicted that if the waywardness of the younger generation did not cease, the state would not be able to complete housing projects since it would be forced to build prisons. However, very little publicity was given to these iconoclastic words of a world famous expert [16]. A little episode, highly illustrative of this 'public philosophy' comes to mind: a probation officer, whom I greatly appreciate because of his natural common sense, consulted me concerning a youngster of 12 who was under his supervision. When I commented that he should first of all see that the boy was at home by eight o'clock and not roaming the streets and disturbing the whole neighbourhood, he replied that this was part of the Israeli 'atmosphere' (way of life). I am not sure if this is an indispensable element of the national 'atmosphere', but I am certain that it is unhealthy and symptomatic of the disorientation of the educators.

The second aspect, and morally probably more detrimental, is a lack of compassion and the absence of consideration for one's fellow man.

Professor Klein, an advisor to the United Nations for social services, stressed that the foremost obstacle in the treatment of social cases was the indifferent and even inimical atmosphere towards all those who are not able to become cogs in the machinery of building and productivity. The government was pressed to return Prof. Klein with maximum speed, and any mention of his report is still taboo (although, in the last years there is a marked improvement in this field).

In accordance with all this, it is not surprising, that, for example, respect of traffic regulations is considered as a sign of cowardice and lack of 'manhood'; it is not by chance that Israel holds the world's record of road accidents - the experts being unanimous in their opinion that the foremost cause therefore is the human factor, the lack of politeness and consideration for the fellow man.

16. It is not my intention to compare here the proportions and forms of juvenile delinquency in Israel and elsewhere. However, the tolerance towards acts of hooliganism in Israel on the part of the authorities is quite unparallelled.

Some additional phenomena of everyday life seem to be directly related to this 'public philosophy'. After the establishment of the state it took ten years or more before a law against air pollution and other nuisances was passed - and this as a private member's bill. After its passage a general obstruction with the authorities as active accomplices followed, and to such an extent that some newspapers raised the question of whether any rule of law still exists in the country [17]. The negative attitude of the authorities cannot solely be explained by the influence from pressure groups (transport cooperatives, etc.) or on the pretext of the expenses involved in the implementation of the law. The obstruction of the regulations commanding orderliness, silence and consideration can be only explained on account of their basic unpopularity because they contradict some sanctified concepts of 'free and uninhibited people living in their free homeland'.

V. Does the Israeli authoritarian personality (similar to his 'classic' model) affirm middle class values? The answer to this question is unequivocally negative. It is however much more difficult to answer the question of what social class does its ideals reflect?

The difficulty stems from at least two sources: the society in Israel (even that of the pre-state period) is in a perpetual flux, due to the technological evolution and the phenomenon of mass-immigration. The tendency of the present development in the polar directions of an affluent society on the one hand, and the so-called 'second Israel' (mostly immigrants from Afro-Asian countries) on the other is quite clear; and also that the ruling class is the *nouveau riche* bureaucracy which masks its conservative interests with a socialist vocabulary.

It seems that the Israeli authoritarian personality does not mirror the values of a definite social class, and surely not of a *stable* one; its genesis seems to be determined more by socio-psychological than by socio-economic factors (the polar negation, by overcompensation of the East-European ghetto, in a manner that preserves many of its original traits, especially the narrow horizons but repainted in another color).

One could venture the idea that the ideals of this personality stem from the affirmation of values of a *pseudo-revolutionary* society [18].

17. In the meantime (i.e. since I lectured on this theme) there was a partial withdrawal of the law on the initiative of the Secretary of Health(!!), who declared that it was not in the interests of the public, but due to pressure from interested groups.
18. This designation is of course a paraphrase of 'pseudo-conservative', although I think that in the USA one deals with real conservatism in cases labelled as 'pseudoconservative'.

Pseudo-revolutionary since:
1. One finds less of the elements affirming revolutionary goals and more of its means: toughness, violence, romanticism and militarism.
2. There are hardly possible revolutionary changes within national boundaries in the mid-twentieth century, and certainly not in a socialist-internationalist sense.
3. Although it entered the epoch of planned economy and nuclear technology, Israeli society has not yet undergone (nor shows any signs of approaching it) the 'ataturkian revolution' of secularization.
4. The dogmatic authority of the collective and the fetishism of its institutions and labour have unmistakable traits of *Religionsersatz*.
5. It is marked by clearly conservative traits; rigid adhesion to ideas and social frameworks which were progressive fifty years ago, opposed to rethink and change outdated ideas and social structures. This opposition stems from naive, nostalgic idealism in some cases, and from the need to safeguard vested interests of enormous parasitic machineries in others.

   As stated repeatedly, the 'revolutionary jump' of healing the Jewish people was, even in the first years of this century blurred by the fatal optical illusion of considering primitive Russian music as the prototype of healthy humanity... although in those years the industrialization and creation of modern industrial societies were already in full progress.

   It is unnecessary to state, that the *anti-intellectualism* of those same romantic agrarian theoreticians of 'healthy humanity' is frankly and unequivocally... contrarevolutionary [19].
6. The unlimited and uninhibited freedom given to youth (and often justified by conceptions of modern psychology) may be revolutionary in the sense of a total negation of patriarchal, authoritarian discipline, but this kind of freedom (without reasonable restrictions and discipline) is but an expression of the insecurity and disorientation of the educators. Romantic nocturnal vagrancy, led by the leader of the youth movement, may easily deteriorate into street corner gang behaviour and antisocial practices euphemistically labelled as 'practical jokes' of the uninhibited youth [20].

19. Appropriate items in a revised F-scale (eg. 'the agricultural worker and military commandant are more important to society than the artist and the professor'), could, at least some years ago so, reveal the affirmation of this pseudo revolutionary ideology.

20. It is illustrative that in the last years some advertisements present pictures of semi-wayward youngsters from the peripheries, assuming that it is this type with whom many of the readers can most easily identify.

In summarising it can be said, that these are values of an economically and socially *unstable* stratum in search of stability, interpreting its ideals in terms of the socialist categories of the beginning of the century, influenced however, more by Tolstoy than by Marx, more by the guerrilla fighter and party-bureaucrat than by the revolutionary intellectual with cosmopolitan horizons.

5. Primitive pollution fears and compulsory premarital ritual*

We build many more Mikvehs than youth centers.

M. K. Shulamith Aloni

* From: 'Forms and Foundations of Israeli Theocracy', Shikpul Press, Tel Aviv, 1968.

I. Purification rituals play a leading role in the life of primitive (pre-literate) societies on the individual and collective level. This applies equally to transition rituals (rite de passage) when the individual or the group prepares itself for the dangerous act of mystic 'death' and rebirth in a new identity (status); to cases of emergence from a state of sacredness and/or pollution because of some perilous contact with the world of the dead or other taboo object; or when dealing with situations where the individual, knowingly or without knowledge, trespassed one of the tribal prohibitions (often sexual in nature), and when the consequent sin and pollution endanger not only the sinner and his neighbours, but the whole tribe.

The purification rituals are often connected with water; with immersion in a river or the 'throwing away' of sins (the pollution, the impurity) into a flowing river. Since water has a cleansing effect, these customs were sometimes rationalised as being on hygienic grounds. Even if there is some truth in it, there is no doubt that hygiene plays only a minor role in those magic rituals. It is enough to point to the fact that the conditions under which the purification is carried out are often rich enough sources of infection and contamination to understand that here one is dealing with 'ritual pollution' and mystic-symbolic purification, and not with a hygienic act. Thus, for example, the immersion of hundreds of thousands of pilgrims in the holy waters of the Ganges, who suffer from a considerable number of different ailments, may be the cause of the spread of disease, and no amount of holy-purifying power of the water will prevent pollution and contagion.

The fear of pollution-contamination reigns in the mind of primitive man, and is the source of the taboos and isolation-laws which ensure the prevention of contact with the impure. Not only direct contact, but also the speech and the look of the impure may pollute not only man and animal, but also the earth and the sun. Taboos of every-day life, purification rituals and sometimes even the establishment of the social hierarchy (for example, in India) are the result of this archaic fear - where proximity or distance from 'pollution-centers' (for example, dead bodies) are the axioms of the social organization.

Of special significance in the danger of pollution and transgression is - blood. It is often considered as the substance of life and therefore, the revenge of the wounded is feared. Life may be endangered by every contact with blood. This danger is the basis for many taboos in general and in the social-erotic sphere, in particular. The whole sexual life is subject to these taboos, and a woman, because of her biological process, is a dangerous being: menstruation, pregnancy, birth and defloration are situations connected with blood or other secretions. It is a fact that in the Middle Ages, blood (and especially that of menstruation) played a prominent part in the fear of dangerous, poisonous, and sometimes even deadly influences, serving also as a potent weapon in all kinds of magical practices.

Prohibitions and customs which are natural to the primitive way of thinking, but grotesque and shocking to the modern mind in a civilized society - are the result of the primeval fear of pollution [1].

The following are examples from Frazer's well-known book:

'In general, we may say that the prohibition to use the vessels, garments, and so forth of certain persons, and the effects supposed to follow an infraction of the rule, are exactly the same whether the person to whom the things belong are sacred or what we might call unclean and polluted. As the garments which have been touched by a sacred chief kill those who handle them, so do the things which have been touched by a menstruous woman. An Australian blackfellow, who discovered that his wife had lain on his blanket at her menstrual period, killed her and died of terror himself within a fortnight. Hence Australian women at these times are forbidden under pain of death to touch anything that man uses, or even to walk on a path that any man frequents. They are also secluded at childbirth, and all vessels used by them during their seclusion are burned. (...)

Among many peoples similar restrictions are imposed on women in childbed and apparently for similar reasons; at such periods women are supposed to be in a dangerous condition which would infect any person or thing they might touch; hence they are put into quarantine until, with recovery of their health and strength the imaginary danger has passed away. Thus, in Tahiti, a woman after childbirth was secluded for a fortnight or three weeks in a temporary hut erected on sacred ground; during the time of her seclusion, she was debarred from touching provisions, and had to be fed by another. Furthermore, if anyone else touched the child at this period, he was subjected to the same restrictions as the mother until the ceremony of her purification had been performed. (...)

But the secretion of childbed is particularly terrible when it is the product of miscarriage, especially a concealed miscarriage. In this case, it is not merely the man who is threatened or killed; it is the whole country; it is the sky itself that suffers. By a curious association of ideas, a physiological fact causes cosmic troubles.'

It is obvious that the act of marriage, by its very nature, as a state of transition (which always requires special preparations and purifications) and by its danger connected with the blood of the virgin, involves various taboos, precautions and suitable rituals (on which much anthro-

---

1. Cf. J. G. Frazer: 'The Golden Bough'; E. Westermarck: 'History of Human Marriage'; S. Freud: 'Totem und Tabu'; B. Malinowski: 'Sexual Life of Savages'; E. O. James: 'Comparative Religion'; A. E. Crawley: 'The Mystic Rose'; R. Caillois: 'L'Homme et le sacré'; J. Trachtenberg: 'Jewish Magic and Superstition'.

pological literature is available). In some tribes, the fear of this dangerous act is so great that it is not the husband, but his father, the magician, or another 'strong' man who carries out the defloration, a custom of which we can still find direct or symbolical remnants in later cultures. As James writes:

'Everywhere marriage is an institution regulated by custom and law 'not to be taken in hand unadvisedly, lightly or wantonly'. Being a holy estate according to the primitive conception of sacredness, it is hedged round with taboos as numerous as they are binding on the two contracting parties and their immediate associates. The supernatural danger supposed to be attached to defloration, so persistently argued by A. E. Crawley, may be an exaggeration in as much as there is considerable prenuptial license in many communities, but, nevertheless, marriage is a taboo-state, and it cannot be denied that many nuptial rites are directed against the imaginary dangers of defloration and the consummation of the union. To ward off evil influences and secure 'blessings', an elaborate installation ceremonial marks the critical juncture in the upward careers of the two individuals and their families, for marriage invariably represents a rise in social status'.

We find these ideas and the pertinent rituals also in the primeval Semitic tribes. There are many taboos and purification rituals, such as those which are connected in particular with the defence against the dangerous touch of the impure (which, incidentally, according to the well-known ambivalence of the sacred and the impure, is also their most potent remedy!), and others that characterize the entrance to and emergence from the state of sacredness.

R. Caillois writes:

'Le livre entier du Lévitique pourrait être commenté de ce point de vue: on constate à chaque verset la même intime connexion du pur et de l'impur'.

II. Proof that the laws of taboo (observed by the ultra-Orthodox) and the premarital purification ritual (which is *practically compulsory* for all in Israel) characterize not only preliterate societies is given in a booklet containing advice to the future wife [2]. The *marriage instructions,* together with 'The ways of life' ('A message to the bride and bridegroom on their day of joy and to every man and woman in Israel') by Rabbi Dr.

---

2. The bride may also receive the same instructions orally, while registering, from the Rabbanite (usually an older woman versed in religious mores) who, after having received all the necessary information about dates of menstruation in the last few months, will give her consent to the proposed wedding date or insist on another, so that it falls in the most fertile period.

Samuel Grienberg, published by the Chief Rabbinate and the Religious Council of Tel Aviv-Jaffa) which the future bride receives while registering, also contains advertisements, not only of clothes, electrical appliances and offers of services, but also of 'Zim', the national shipping company; all these are additional proof of the mixture in Israel of the Bronze Age, in which these laws of taboos are combined with the Age of Technology of our time.

The following quotations from Rabbi Dr. Grienberg are almost in toto (that there may be no suspicion of a biased choice) except for the long introduction (Part A) written in an apologetic-chauvinistic style, such as: 'It is the exemplary laws of purity of the Jewish family that have aroused the envy of the Gentiles, and that have safeguarded the existence of the Jewish people.' Names of physicians and their publications are mentioned praising these customs, including statements that the male needs two weeks to recuperate.

Sayings of the Sages:

'God said if thou art careful at the time of impurity, you make me grant you a happy life' (Baraithe Middah).

'Shammai said: Great is the woman who observes the laws of the days of menstruation, keeping away from sin she comes near to Paradise.' (Baraithe Middah)

'The clever one among women says: This is your reward, for a little pleasure will you lose your eternal life?' (Paths of Faith)

'Thou shalt not approach her. It has been taught which restriction the Bible has made for the period of menstruation.' It is said: 'And a woman in her impurity, do not approach to sleep with her'. (Aboth d' Rabbi Nathan, 82)

'And you have been warned. R. Josiah said: From this we deduce a warning to the children of Israel that they should separate from their wives near their periods.' (Shevuoth, 18).

'It once happened that a certain scholar who had studied much Bible and Mishnah and had served scholars much, yet died in middle age. His wife took his tefillin and carried them about in synagogues and schoolhouses and complained to them: It is written in the Torah, for that is thy life, and the length of thy day; my husband who read (Bible), learned (Mishnah), and served scholars much, - why did he die in middle age? And no man could answer her. On one occasion, I was a guest at her house, and she related the whole story to me. Said I to her, 'My daughter! How was he to thee in thy days of menstruation?' 'God forbid!' she said. 'He did not touch me even with his little finger.' 'And how was he to thee in thy days of white (garments)?' 'He ate with me, drank with me and slept with me in bodily contact, and it did not occur to him to do other.' Said I

to her, 'Blessed be the Omnipotent for slaying him, that He did not condone on account of the Torah! For lo! the Torah has said, And thou shalt not approach unto woman as long as she is impure by her uncleanness.' (Seder Eliyahu Rabba, Sabbath 13).
(Abridged version according to the English translation)

Laws for the menstrual period and ritual bath

'Also thou shalt not approach unto a woman to uncover her nakedness, as long as she is put apart for her uncleanness'. (Lev. 18.19)

a. A woman seeing a drop of blood, even no bigger than a mustard seed, emerging from her is impure. There is no difference whether she has seen the blood at her fixed time which in the way of woman is called 'menses' without any special examination, or whether she found traces of blood at a different time after examination. The menstruating woman is forbidden to her husband, 'cut off', as is written in the Bible: 'and both of them shall be cut off from among their people' (Lev. 20.18). She is forbidden until after five days of having been clean she has taken a ritual bath (immersed in a mikveh); then she counts seven clean days (as will be explained in the following paragraphs e, f, g).

b. A woman feeling her womb open, as at the period of her menstrual flow, has to examine herself whether the blood is about to flow.

c. The examination must be done with the help of a piece of clean, white cloth. If she finds the cloth covered with reddish or blackish spots, she is impure. Even if after the examination she does not see anything on the cloth she is impure, for we say, a drop of blood like a mustard seed coming out of her, and she is impure, because her womb has certainly not opened without reason. But if the cloth (or the witness, as it was called by the sages, blessed be their memory) is white (a white or green fluid), which also comes from the source, then she is pure, and when there is any doubt, the rabbi has to be asked for advice.

d. A woman finding a stain on her flesh or on her dress or on the linen of her bed, in spite of not having felt anything, must show the stain to the rabbi if it looks reddish, or blackish or golden, and if the rabbi says that it is impure, all the laws for the menstrual period are binding upon her.

e. A woman who has become impure after having seen blood or a stain, must wait five days, that means - from the day of her seeing it and four more days, and on the fifth day at dusk she examines herself once again at the end of the day, and if she finds nothing red she makes a cessation of the purification and from the next day on counts seven clean days. The 'cessation of purification' must be made close before sunset.

f. The cessation of purification is made thus: She must wash herself well, at least in this place, put on a clean, white shirt; she must spread a clean, white sheet on her bed, examine whether the pillows and covers are also clean; after that, she has to take a piece of clean, white linen or of old cotton wool and to insert this piece as far as her hand reaches, turn it to all sides, then take it out and examine in daylight whether it is reddish or blackish. The cessation of purification cannot be made earlier than at the end of the fifth day after the beginning of seeing. There is no difference whether she saw blood on all the five days and it stopped only at the end of the fifth day, of whether she saw it on only one day.

From the next day on, after the examination of the 'cessation of purification', finding herself completely clean, she begins counting seven clean days. On all the seven clean days, she must examine herself twice on each day, once in the morning and the second time at the end of the day, in the evening. These examinations are also made with a piece of clean, white cloth, as described above. If it is hard for her to do it every day, she may examine herself thoroughly on only the first and seventh day of the days of counting, and on the other days she may examine herself only lightly.

If she did not examine herself on even one day of the clean days (except for the examination of the 'cessation of purification') and made only a light examination, the seven clean days cannot be reckoned at all, and the 'cessation of purification' is as if not made at all.

g. The seven clean days must be successive; that means, on all these days she must not find any blood or stain. And if she saw something reddish or blackish or found a stain on one of the seven days, the counting of the former days is null, and she must cease the purification and begin counting seven other clean days.

At the end of the seven clean days, she must take a kosher ritual bath at night and will then be pure, but no bathtub or shower are able to remove the impurity of menstruation and ward off the mortally dangerous taboo, as it is said in the Bible, for those can by no means replace a ritual bath according to the law of the Bible.

On all the days of her menstruation, also on the seven clean days, the man and the woman are forbidden to touch each other, to hand over things from one to the other, and they must avoid coming close and expressions of love. This distance must be kept as long as the woman has not taken a kosher mikveh.

h. On the day on which the date for her wedding is fixed, the bride must make a 'cessation of purification' and from the next day count seven clean days (as described above in paragraphs f and g), and after this she has to take a kosher ritual bath in the evening. She should take the bath as close to the wedding day as possible (at any rate, the bath should not be taken more than four days before the wedding night).

i. If the wedding day is postponed, the rabbi should be asked for advice on how to behave.

j. A bride who is compelled to take the bath on the seventh day and cannot take it in the evening must ask the rabbi for advice.

k. A bride who could not take the bath before the wedding day, or who saw also after the bath, and the wedding had to be celebrated at the period of impurity, is forbidden to her husband until she is purified, and they are forbidden to be alone together.

l. The man who has married a virgin must leave her alone immediately after the fulfilment of the precept, and on the fourth day (other women on the fifth day) at dusk she has to make a 'cessation of purification' according to the law as mentioned above (paragraph f) and to count seven clean days beginning from the fifth day of marriage.

Laws for the ritual bath (immersion)

m. The ritual bath is to be taken at night just after the appearance of the stars, and even if, for some reason, she could not take the bath at the appointed time and has to take the bath on the day following the night of the ritual bath, as on the fifth or ninth day of counting, she has to take the bath at night and not during the day.

n. If, through no fault of hers, she could not take the ritual bath at night, she is allowed to bathe on the day following the night of the ritual bath, for example, on the eighth day, but she must bring her case before the rabbi who, finding her reason valid, will allow her to take the ritual bath during the day.

o. Before taking the ritual bath, the woman must wash herself thoroughly in hot water, paying special attention to folds and hidden places, and she must examine her whole body lest there remain something sticking to her body that divides. She has to pare the nails of her fingers and toes and to comb her hair carefully. She must clean herself between the fingers and the toes, brush her teeth lest there remain something to pick. Those who have teeth which can be taken out of the mouth must take them out during the ritual bath. After the washing, she must rinse her body with hot water from top to toe, and see if she is completely clean. On the day before the ritual bath she must not eat meat; only on Saturday and feastdays is it allowed, and she must pick her teeth clean after the meal. Between washing and taking the ritual bath, she must be careful not to get dirty, and she is not allowed to eat anything.

p. The washing must begin while there is still daylight close to the time of the ritual bath; she must, therefore, begin washing while there is still daylight (that is at the end of the seventh day), and will busy herself with it until after the appearance of the stars. Immediately after washing, she should take the ritual bath, but if it is impossible for her to do it the same night, she may do so at the end of the next day, but she must examine her body again thoroughly before the ritual bath.

If she cannot wash at the ritual bath-house, being compelled to wash at another place, she must take with her a comb and comb her hair again in the ritual bath-house before taking the ritual bath.

q. After having taken off her clothes, the woman must dip her whole body at once in the ritual bath until the water covers her whole body and her hair, and there must not be anything dividing on her body; she must also take off her rings and ear-rings before the ritual bath.

She must not dip standing erect and not in a sitting position, and not swimming and not too much bent. She must dip slightly, swimming, making movements like a woman kneading bread. She must bite her lips with a slight pressure and her hands and feet should move as if she were going to the market; they should not be pressed to her body and not each other, she may either open or close her eyes.

During the bath, a Jewish woman, at least more than twelve years old, must stand near her, to see that the water covers her body and her hair entirely. If she has no one to stand near her, she must bind her hair in a net so that her hair does not spread in the water. A woman who cannot dip by herself must be held by her friend, this friend shall put her hands into the water of the ritual bath and hold her without force.

r. After the dipping but while she is still in the water, she must pronounce the blessing: Blessed art thou our Lord, King of the world, who has hallowed us by His commandments and commanded us to take the ritual bath. After this, the woman used to dip a second time so that the blessing is between the first and the second dipping.

s. At the end of the seven clean days, it is her duty to take the ritual bath without postponement, if her husband is in town.

t. A woman may take the ritual bath on Friday night and on a holiday if she could not take it before.

u. If the time of the bath falls on the evening after the Sabbath (or on the evening after a holiday) she must wash and clean herself on the eve of the Sabbath (or the holiday) by daylight, and on the evening after the Sabbath (or the holiday) she must wash and clean herself again in hot water, before taking the ritual bath, paying attention that there is nothing dividing on her body.

v. A woman after confinement is like a menstruating woman according to the law of the Bible. If she has given birth to a son, she must wait a week, and if to a daughter, two weeks, and will then make a 'cessation of purification', count seven clean days and then take the ritual bath like all women purifying themselves after their menstruation.

w. All the matters of the ritual bath have to be done with patience and tranquility.

x. Finally, we mention the law of abstinence close to the period of menstruation when the woman has her menstruation at a fixed time (if the menstruation is not at a fixed time or if it is irregular, she must ask the rabbi for advice). Every woman who has her menstruation at a fixed time, seeing it, for example, every thirty days, or every twenty-eight days, is forbidden to her husband, whether she is used to see that it is the time of her menstruation in the morning, at noon, or at the end of the day. In the night before and in the night after (when she saw nothing on the fixed day of menstruation) she is allowed. And if she is used to see in the night (for example, she always sees in the night before the thirtieth day) whether seeing it at the beginning of the night, at midnight or at the end of the night, she is forbidden to her husband throughout the whole night, but she is allowed before and after; although there are those who restrict themselves to abstinence the night before the day it is time to see, and when it is time to see in the night, they keep away the day before.

A pregnant woman after three months, as well as a nursing woman during all the twenty-four months after the birth does not expect her menstruation as usual. But if she has again seen, she has to expect it like menstruation that does not function regularly.

After the period of pregnancy and nursing, she has to expect her first menstruation as she was used to before.

A middle-aged woman whose menstruation has stopped, not having seen anything for three periods, is considered clean of blood.

y. Apart from all the laws which are given here in a very concise form, there exist, of course, many more laws concerning this subject. Thus, for example, there are laws concerning the various kinds of menstruation which are not regular, or a woman who does not menstruate at all; also a woman who sees blood following sexual intercourse, an abortion; or a woman who, after the ritual bath, found something dividing on her body; a woman suffering from a rash, furuncles or the like. In such matters and similar ones, a rabbi must always be asked for advice or, as one usually says: one should consult a scholar.

III. We shall not enter into discussion here with the opinions of the learned rabbi - as a rationalistic discussion with ideas based on pre-logic-magic thinking (which produced these taboos and rituals) would be even more grotesque than these primeval conceptions. They are absurd for the modern mind, whether one considers the reason for the death of the husband whose wife did not observe the commands of the taboo, or the necessity to ask the rabbi for advice in cases of doubt, or the claim that it is precisely those taboos which safeguarded the existence of the nation (it would be more acceptable if this claim were made, as it is often done, in relation to the racial-segregatory laws forbidding intermarriage for the sake of 'the purity of the people'). As to the purification laws in general, the examples in the first paragraph demonstrate sufficiently that these taboos are not unique to Judaism. Some other primitive tribes went even further in the seclusion laws for the woman during her biological processes.

Whether the withdrawal of the young husband from his wife at the moment of defloration protects his life - is doubtful. But there is certainly no doubt that this practice does not contribute to the joyful experience of the couple on their wedding night. The argument that 'the man also needs two weeks to restore his strength' - seems to us somewhat pessimistic - if it applies to a man in the first sixty years of his life...

In this context we want, however, to deal with the influence of the obligation to undergo the purification ritual before marriage of young Israeli women, as the visit to the Mikveh (ritual bath) is a nightmare and sometimes a serious traumatic experience for a large number of them.

While it is not possible to enforce the observance of these archaic taboos, the orthodox Rabbinate has the possibility to exert illegal pressure by threatening not to conduct the marriage ceremony, thus forcing girls to undergo the purification ritual in the Mikveh.

The following are excerpts from interviews with young women about their experience in connection with the 'obligatory counselling' and the purification ritual. (For two of the interviews, I am indebted to the psychologist, Mrs. Mishkinski).

1. T, 26 years old (21 years old at the time of her visit to the Mikveh), in the country since age 7, secondary school graduate, housewife.

A gay, open woman, giving the impression of a person with an outstanding emotional stability. Mother of two children. She is not religious, but not at all anti-religion. She would have liked to have had the opportunity of a civil marriage and a religious ceremony. She explains that although she is not religious, she thinks that the ritual and mystery of the marriage ceremony add to the importance of the occasion, and this mystery also increases the responsibility towards marriage. She thinks that this is superior to 'just the signature before the clerk', though she cannot explain why.

The experience in the Mikveh, she describes as the most repellent and disgusting experience of her life. She was surprised to hear that it was unlawful to compel her to go to the Mikveh; neither she nor any of her friends knew this. She thought that the rabbi had the right to refuse to conduct the marriage ceremony if she did not bring written confirmation from the Mikveh.

From her friends, she had heard of the dirt in the ritual bath-houses, and she went there (together with her neighbour) already with a feeling of repulsion and anger at the fact that she was *compelled* to go; that her privacy was invaded; that she was forced to undergo a ritual in which she did not believe and to which, in her opinion, no one had the right to force her.

The Mikveh itself was not as unhygienic as she had expected, but the woman who attended to her seemed quite dirty (she made a movement with her hands as if her fingers were sticky). After answering that she knew the biological meaning of married life, and according to her wish the 'Rabbanite' refrained from giving her sexual explanations. She herself pared her nails, but later on the old woman carefully examined her fingers and her toes. Being touched by her aroused a feeling of disgust, and the whole situation - her sitting naked in front of the repellent old woman, was accompanied by a feeling of shame and loathing. (She had never felt a similar shame in front of a physician or when she had to undress at the recruiting station). The 'Rabbanite' paid special attention to her hair, also, while she was in the Mikveh, even hurting her, for she was pulling it. [3]

The experience of dipping was most disagreeable. She was under the impression that she was brutally pushed into deep water, and when she got water in her ears (to which she is especially sensitive) she touched the walls of the Mikveh in terror and because of that, she did not repeat the words of the old woman correctly, who therefore dipped her in the water seven times, instead of three.

Coming out, she had only one wish - to get home and to take a bath in a clean bath-tub, for she felt dirty all over.

2. M, 26 years old. She too is a 'Sabra born abroad' (she came to Israel at the age of three), has an academic education, is well-balanced, very self-confident. She works at an institute for scientific research. 'When I went to the Rabbanite, I had already made up my mind *not* to go to the Mikveh. Also, my friends who work together with me did not go there, and they pass on the name of some rabbi who does not demand a certificate from the Mikveh. I was only interested in getting married on the fixed date, as we intended to go on a journey abroad immediately afterwards. I prepared, therefore, all the relevant answers as to the dates of the menstruation in the last few months, lest she oppose the proposed date.'

'When I entered the room of the 'Rabbanite', I saw in my file that the name of the institute where I work was underlined in red. It may be that this was of some influence. Answering her question of whether I was traditionally educated with a definite 'No', she asked, without looking at me, the dates, but did not offer explanations of the 'facts of life' and the duties of the married woman. She acknowledged the date, handed me the booklet, and this was all.'

3. P, 32 years old, was the only one of all the interviewed women who remembered her visit to the Mikveh as a pleasant experience. This was

---

3. As to the treatment of hair, Cf. the underlying element of demonological fear in the cited work of Trachtenberg.

her first marriage and, although she was not questioned about it, the interviewer, who had known her for a long time, was of the opinion that, in spite of her age, she did not have sexual relations before her marriage.

She was born in South America, had a secondary education, immigrated 7 years ago, works as a clerk. P is not religious. She describes herself as 'emotional' and having an optimistic attitude toward life. She tells about the 'episode' with a sense of humor. The meeting with the 'Rabbanite' shocked her; although she was prepared for the questions, the indiscretion of prying into her intimate life hurt her feelings of decency. 'No one has the right to do so'. She threw the booklet into the wastepaper basket without reading it.

P. went to the Mikveh a day before the wedding, 'in a rather hysterical mood', according to her words. There, she was pleasantly surprised, for in contrast to those her friends went to, this one was clean and pleasant. She was alone, there was no other woman at that time. The 'Instructress' told her to call her when she was in the water and left the room while she undressed, and did not examine her hair and nails. Descending the steps and going slowly into the warm water, she had a very pleasant feeling, and she experienced something which she calls 'mystical'. [4]

She had never experienced anything like this before. She did not call the woman immediately; she did so only after having crossed the pool a few times. After this, the woman dipped her three times and the feeling of mystery increased. She returned home relaxed and in a mood of euphoria.

4. A, 25 years old, a new immigrant from Yugoslavia, married to a senior civil servant of the Ministry of Foreign Affairs; academic education.

'I do not want to recall it at all. It is hard to decide whether the dominant sensation was repulsion (when she touched my nails), madness (when she told me to go to the rabbi in case of illness), or ludicrousness (when she began explaining about sex-life). I felt a strong urge to tell her of my former boyfriends... but I controlled myself for the sake of finishing as quickly as possible. Such madness in the twentieth century!'

In the talks with reliable, educated Orthodox people about the prevalent customs of going to the Mikveh and the observance of the purifi-

---

[4]. The experience which P. correctly calls mystical certainly is based on a feeling of ego-dissolution and a blurring of the usual physical boundaries while entering the water, which changes the habitual constancy of the I-External World perception.

cation laws in sexual life, two contradictory versions were given: according to the first, intellectual, religious women also strictly observe the customs; according to the second version, there is a general tendency to evade them, even in the religious kibbutzim, where sharp control and criticism by public opinion exist. [5]

The coercion to undergo the prescribed ritual in the Mikveh reveals not only one of the least aesthetic aspects of religious pressure, but the ruthless requirement to fulfil the commandment, without even being much disturbed by the lack of persuasion of the individual reveals, on the one hand, the same deeply irrational beliefs that the water of the Mikveh is really different from any other bath, and that death was actually caused by a transgression of abstinence commandments and, on the other hand, the valuation of the importance of *practice* as against that of *subjective belief*.

The emphasis on obedience and formal ritual against belief is characteristic of the stage of religious development where 'magic technology' is of much greater significance than belief (and where the influence is postulated as automatic because of the action itself). The attitude of the Orthodox authorities in their dogmatic demand for the observance of the commands, even without belief, reflects this stage of development. There is, of course, also some hope that doing will lead to believing - which is well-founded only if there is complete control of the whole way of life when the ever-recurring automation of ritual prevents the awakening of doubt. But this state of coercion has not yet been reached.

An additional important factor in understanding these relations and especially of the coercive legalistic spirit with its total disregard of personal belief:

The petrified Jewish orthodoxy (like the Catholic orthodoxy) did not develop in the last few hundred years, and its whole make-up suits the authoritarian, dogmatic structure of the religions before the Reformation (and the Renaissance); that means, before the appearance of the modern *individual* with his demands for individual rights of belief (or disbelief) and of personal interpretation of the Holy Scriptures and freedom of behaviour according to his individual conscience. [6]

---

5. About observance of the above-mentioned laws by traditional women, Cf. R. Bechi - J. Matros: Contraception and Induced Abortions Among Jewish Maternity Cases in Israel, McMillan Research Fund Quarterly.
6. Although there were early statements repudiating the ways of the Orthodox establishment it was only in mid 1966 that one could witness the first organized initiative of orthodox intellectuals (led by Prof. E. Urbach of Jerusalem's Hebrew University) to create a movement (Judaism of the Torah) with the aim of foster-

Orthodox Jewry does not recognize individual belief as a right, being very straightforward about it. The religion of Israel is in its opinion and according to its definition, a religion of the *nation* (the Bible was given to the *people)*; it is a religion of the collective which has full right to impose upon the individual, rituals and force upon him the commands and prohibitions of Jehovah, the jealous God.

ing religious values by persuasion and opposing coercion through religious legislation, and also an attempt to liberate the religious realm from the monopoly of party machines. The movement is fiercely opposed by all the Orthodox parties and 'Hazofe', organ of the NRP, even refused to print a paid announcement about its founding convention.

6. Two stereotypes of the national mythology: the Sabra superman and the inferior Diaspora Jew *

* Paper, delivered to the congress of IPA, Jerusalem, 1964. From: 'Research on Patterns of Tolerance and Intolerance', Shikpul Press, Tel Aviv, 1969 (in co-operation with D. Ben-Zwi).

Some years ago, after an outbreak of violence by Jerusalem youth, the Hebrew daily 'Haaretz' published an editorial entitled 'Our Charming Sabras'. This critical article, which posed some soul-searching questions concerning the character of the Sabras 'whom we have idolized', verged on sacrilege.

The predominant attitude in all walks of life in Israel, both in the written and spoken language, tends to raise the Sabra to an idol-like stature and a superman. This begins in the kindergarten, with tales in which the Sabras are depicted as *free and proud,* in contrast to their inferior parents from the Diaspora; right through to standardized advertisement pictures depicting them as athletic boys and girls in uniform or in shorts. This ideology is mirrored in an anecdote the new immigrant learns soon after his arrival, in his Ulpan [1] textbook concerning a tourist who jokingly tells a little boy that he would be prepared to buy him, and receives the following answer: 'No, don't buy me, but my little brother. He was born in this country, and is a real Sabra'. This attitude is also reflected in characters presented in newspapers and in Hebrew literature, in letters to editors and articles in which complaints about the impolite behaviour of youngsters and their arrogance towards non-Israeli Jews are rejected on the grounds that this kind of behaviour is due to a (desirable) lack of inhibitions and positive national pride. Then there are also works of so-called 'art' such as the novel 'Exodus' [2] whose heroes and happenings are exploited by tourist offices, remoulding the years of the establishment of the State so as to fit the melodramatic story.

The opposite of the Sabra 'superman' is the 'Diaspora Jew', the symbol of a weak, unwanted, inferior and almost despicable being. This attitude too is expressed in books in which small children are told how happy they should be not to be such an inferior type, and it is found again in the doctrines of politicians and educationalists who, by a 'slight' distortion of history, negate the past of Jewish dispersion - regarded as something to be ashamed of - and fabricate a direct link between the generation of Sabras and the Biblical heroic period. This same trend is reflected in some figures of present-day Hebrew literature.

And with what scorn Israeli youth reacts to the alleged faint-heartedness of the six million victims of Nazism!

It is evident that, in an exploration of stereotypes, it is not the task

---

1. Ulpan - Hebrew language courses sponsored by the authorities for new immigrants and inhabitants not familiar with the language.
2. Novel by Leon Uris, published 1958, describing the illegal immigration from Europe as background to Israel's War of Liberation - in romantic, heroic terms.

of research to assess to what extent any stereotype image fits reality; every generalisation contains some degree of truth and some of fallacy. A prejudice is thus named not because it is wholly false but because it claims to apply to all those belonging to a certain category or group.

However, the well-known fact that stereotypes tend to turn into self-fulfilling prophecies - especially the *socially desirable ones* which become 'binding' while the negative ones may be only imposed - raises a psychological, social and educational problem which requires further research. It is also evident that nothing is easier than to convince someone that he is a superior being, particularly if the self-image of this superman is characterized, in addition to physical strength (the attainment of which requires effort) by primitiveness and single-mindedness (which do not require any special effort) as esteemed traits.

If aggressiveness, loudness, ignorance of basic international expressions, and fascination with arms are held to be grounds for pride, then, of course, all these compel the child to prove that he is not a 'ghetto-type' by, for example, speaking to the teacher impertinently; taken to its extremity, this attitude has found expression in the case of the Sabra-girl (mentioned elsewhere) who posed, naked with a sten-gun, as a candidate for Hollywood - in order to resemble the national archetype.

Our study of the two most important stereotypes of the national mythology originally contained two parts: an experimental part in which the self-image of the Sabras and their conception of the 'Diaspora-Jew' are examined, and a content analysis of literary and similar texts. [3]

1. THE EXPERIMENT

Using the technique of story-completion, described in paragraphs 2 and 10, we examined 512 Sabras (175 boys and 337 girls) aged 15-22; in four groups:
I.   High-school students from the second and third grades in the Tel Aviv area (144 boys; 247 girls), (including group **Ia, see below**).
II. Students of the same age-group in Kibbutzim in Galilee (16 boys and 11 girls).
III. Students of the same grade in religious high schools in the central area of the country (4 boys and 4 girls).
IV. Students (mostly girls) at a teachers' seminary in the Tel Aviv area (11 boys; 75 girls).

3. In this version, the latter part has been excluded (Ed.).

Among the students examined was a group of 12% not born in Israel but educated there since early childhood (they will be called 'Sabras born abroad').

We assumed that it was possible to include in the category of 'Sabras' all those who, from early childhood had lived in Israel, and we expected to find in them an even greater measure of identification with and adoration of the 'Sabra-traits' (according to the principle that the proselyte is more Catholic than the Pope... if such a comparison can be made here).

This fact was found to be true in the case of some of the examinees, but not all. The question - which factors are influential in causing identification or non-identification with the 'Sabra-traits' - is still an open one, and many variables may play an important part. Apart from the factor of the age at which the children came to the country, great importance has also to be attached to the way in which they were received by those born in the country; to the degree of identification or non-identification with their parents and the parents' relationship to the Sabras, and to the status or the parents' ethnic sub-group etc. - a subject worthy of further examination.

Because of the small size of this group, the reliability of the Sabras' self-image has not been influenced and even allows for certain interesting analyses.

The examinees wrote either about their own sex or about the opposite sex.

In the largest group (which includes Ia) we made a detailed content analysis and a quantitative list of the traits mentioned; in the other groups, we only made a survey of the compositions by inspection. The first group wrote about the Sabra: 177 stories - 86 on the masculine and 91 on the feminine type; 214 compositions were written about the Diaspora Jew - 102 about the masculine and 112 about the feminine type.

We drew up a list of one hundred traits of the Sabra, each of which was mentioned at least three times, and a total of 723 traits relating to the masculine, and 832 to the feminine character. Certain traits are mentioned repeatedly, appearing in almost every other story (45%), while the ratio of the first item to the 15th on the list, which we have included in the hierarchical image of the stereotype is 4 : 1.

In the analysis of the stories about the Diaspora Jew, we found 69 items that appeared at least three times each, out of a total of 470 items concerning the male and 413 concerning the female. The ratio between the first item of the stereotype list (mentioned in nearly 60% of the stories) and the last is 5 : 1.

2. STORIES ABOUT THE SABRA

From the story: 'The Way of Chaim'

The conversation was animated. Someone said: 'I would like to know Chaim's opinion.' At this moment Chaim entered and sat down. Chaim was a typical Sabra.

Continue this sentence and describe Chaim as fully as possible.

I. (A girl 15½ years old)
Continuation of the sentence: The company ('gang') listened to Chaim's opinion on the subject. Some agreed, a few opposed him. Chaim, as you know, is a typical Sabra. Typical character-traits of 'Sabrahood' are:

1. Bragging ('Show-off') - The Sabras are convinced that they are better than anybody else. The fact that they are impolite, free and impertinent in their behaviour makes them appear arrogant.
2. Sabras are not snobs - they don't mind standing in the street talking to one another, playing with youngsters of different communities (here the respondent mainly had the younger generation, those born in the '50s and '60s in mind).
3. They are terribly impolite - which, however, does not detract from them, but adds a specific dimension to their personality. Because of this lack of politeness they excel in...
4. Sincerity - youngsters of our 'gang' are ready to discuss any subject and to speak their mind frankly without bothering 'what impression' they make.
5. The Sabras are free and sociable, they like company and like a chat.
6. The Sabras like to let themselves go. They are good mixers (not 'soap' in Hebrew slang).
7. The Sabras are very gay, enjoy life, know how to make merry at the right time (those I know, members of the youth-movement, are like that, at any rate).
8. Patriotism - many Sabras would never consider emigrating to affluent countries.
9. Outward cynicism and inner sentimentality - the Sabras like to ridicule ideals and ideas outwardly, but on the other hand, they think the old people are quite right to admonish them about pioneering, security, the need for farmers and the like.
10. They hate to study (most of them anyway). 'Bookworm' or 'professor' are very insulting names to call a Sabra. Summary: The human

Sabras resemble the Sabra-plant - on the outside they are prickly and inside somewhat soft.

From the story: 'The Way of Daliah'

The conversation was animated. Someone said: 'I would like to know Daliah's opinion. At that moment Daliah entered and sat down. Daliah was a typical Sabra.

II. (A girl 15½ years old)
Daliah was a tall and slim girl with one thick black braid. She sat down, a look of some arrogance was in her eyes. She was gay and laughed all the time, joking with her neighbour. Everyone liked Daliah, although she was cheeky, like most Sabra-girls and rather boastful.

She had a lot of self-confidence, always knew what she wanted and generally got it.

These were, in general, the characteristic traits visible to all. But, underneath the layer of 'boastfulness' and self-confidence we also find a sensitive and good soul, ready to help others. She was unaffected, not particularly coquettish or conceited. She always spoke straight to the point and without hesitation.

On the whole, such is a typical Sabra, but there are always exceptions to the rule.

3. THE STIMULUS, THE SYMBOL IT CONTAINS AND THE REACTION OF THE RESPONDENTS

The technique of story-completion was chosen for the exploration of the stereotypes because, in our opinion, this method stimulates more vivid descriptions than the check-list method which furnishes a basically quantitative list of fragmented traits, with pre-fixed items, which has been justly criticized by S. Asch. The choice was made in spite of the fact that the 'deciphering' of the traits from the stories and the quantitative break-down of the items involves much more work.

As to the content of the stimulus: the scene of a friendly social chat was chosen because a) similar scenes (the 'kumsitz' [4], etc.) are almost archetypical for the local way of life; and b) in the psycho-therapeutic

4. Kumsitz: barbecue-sing-song kind of informal party, outdoors around the campfire.

work of one of us, perhaps the most recurrent statement (to illustrate the complaint) was 'I want to be like all of them'; 'I have difficulties in participating in the conversations of the 'gang'.'

The stimulus-scene may have been perhaps somewhat suggestive in its contents as to the traits of 'influential' and 'well-liked', and in some stories it has indeed been pointed out that there is a hint in the text that Chaim was an important personality, since the others were so interested in his opinion (although in the stimulus only one said so). On the other hand, we also found 'projective' explanations of the stimulus as, for example, one person who said that the text already made it clear that Chaim was impolite, since it says that he entered and sat down but it is not mentioned that he greeted anyone.

If there was any doubt about the influence of the stimulus (in its context) it disappeared entirely in the next stage of the examination, after the same story (serving also as a control for the influence of the stimulus) was given with the final sentence that 'Chaim was a typical Diaspora-Jew' (Ia) and in which the above items were mentioned in only very few stories.

One can thus draw the conclusion: although it is generally true, as Asch points out (in connection with stereotypes Sodhi and Bergius repeat the finding) that the meaning of an expression changes according to its context, the expressions *'Sabra'* and *'Diaspora Jew'* are so heavily charged with emotion that the various contexts do not influence them, and they can be considered as 'labels of primary potency' (Allport).

On the other hand, the stimulus already contains a stereotype - the conventional symbol of 'Sabra', and in quite a number of stories the symbol was referred to in its stereotyped meaning.

In the illustration of the stimulus sentence, the respondents often not only described the Sabra - but used his type also for an ideological discussion on the theme of how the Sabra was and how he should be.

It is remarkable, particularly since the compositions were anonymous, that there was almost a 100% rejection of the stereotype. Perhaps an even stronger proof than the content of most stories, on the existence of the stereotype in the meaning of the 'superman' (i.e. that the designation Sabra is not only applied to a person born or growing up in Israel, but that it also depicts him as possessing superior traits) can be found in a few texts in which the opinion is expressed that the typical Sabra no longer exists. These texts, even in group IV [5] are accompanied by a

---

5. In group IV, after writing the stories, the subjects were asked whether they had described a real, literary or imaginary person. The majority answered that

guilt-feeling at not having fulfilled the norm of the national ego-ideal.

As for the presence of the stereotype, it is, of course, quite irrelevant if some students thought that they *had* to write in a certain way - in accordance with the official image of the archetype - even if they were not quite honest or that the deviation from he conventional image had to be commented upon. (For example: 'Daliah, although a Sabra, was polite and well brought-up').

It was interesting to see that in one class, the task was received with mocking laughter, but as one of the stories we mentioned proves, this laughter contained much of self-defence.

In the majority of stories a complete or almost complete identification with the Sabra can be discerned and the wish to be a typical Sabra was expressed in the following remark: 'Chaim represented the lovable Sabra whom everyone would like to resemble'.

For critical remarks about the Sabra see the following paragraph.

In many cases the Sabra described is of the same age as the writer, or a little older (in most cases the Sabra-boy or girl are members of a youth-movement). In only a few stories was the person described as an adult, and in some descriptions it is stressed that he belonged to the former generation.

4. THE STEREOTYPE OF THE SABRA

The content analysis of the descriptions of the stories reveals the following hierarchical structure within the stereotyped image:

The Sabra (She)
Appearance
1. Tall
2. 'Blorit' (a 'naturalistic' hair-do)
3. Strong and hardy
4. Tanned

5. Light-coloured eyes
6. Freckled
7. Hair: blonde or black

The Sabra (He)
Appearance
1. Charming
2. Good-looking
3. Slender
4. Hair: a) black; b) blonde; c) brunette. One long plait
5. Tall
6. Tanned (and freckled)
7. Light-coloured eyes

they had described a real person, or one based on reality. When talking about the 'Diaspora-Jew', many subjects based their description on literature, such as the works of Y. L. Gordon, Mendele Mocher Sfarim and Shalom Aleichem, although the person to be described was a contemporary one. (The same happened with group Ia.)

Clothes
Negligent simplicity (or simplicity)
Sandals, slacks, 'tembel' hat.

Clothes
Simple (negligent simplicity)
Slacks, sandals.

Personality
1. Dynamic (alert, stormy)
2. Aggressive (assertive, rebellious)
3. Ill-mannered
4. Arrogant and boastful
5. Patriotic
6. Influential
7. Impudent
8. Well-liked, high status
9. Kind-hearted
10. Serious and reasonable
11. Bright and clever
12. Free
13. Sincere
14. Pioneering
15. Cynical (and has a sense of humour)

Personality
1. Dynamic
2. Bright and clever
3. Influential
4. Gay
5. Kind-hearted
6. Well-liked, high status
7. Impudent
8. Arrogant and boastful
9. Serious and reasonable
10. Aggressive (resolute)
11. Sincere
12. Patriotic
13. Free
14. Pioneering
15. Ill-mannered

As these stereotypes are a combination of the self-image (i.e. of the same sex), and the opinions of the opposite sex, the following remarks may be added:

1. Whereas there is full agreement between boys and girls as to the description of the girl's clothes, there is a reversal of the first and second item in the description of the boys's clothes when described by a boy (self-description): negligent simplicity gets the second place in the hierarchy. Its first place in the hierarchy is therefore influenced by the girls' evaluation.

2. The boys value first and foremost strength and physical health in their own sex (themselves). This trait appears at the top of their list, whereas the girls give it a middle position.

3. The boys consider charm important when they describe **girls and put** it at the top of the list, while the girls mention it among the last items.

4. The girls, on their part, prefer 'tall and slim' which in the description of girls by girls (themselves) occupies the first place, but is not mentioned by the boys. The girls, remaining consistent with this difference, value the tallness of the Sabra-girl, which is therefore included in the

general stereotype, although it is missing from the stereotype of the boys where their height is given as medium or average, coming last in the list. The boys are satisfied with medium height for the Sabra-girl, although they demand tallness from their own sex, whereas the girl remains consistent with the appraisal of height in both sexes, preferring the adjectives 'tall and slim' for girls and 'tall' for the opposite sex.

5. The boys do not specify the colour of eyes and hair in the description of their own sex. Only once is colour of hair given by boys. In contrast they expect light-coloured eyes and fair or brunette hair in Sabra-girls. The girls, however, expect light-coloured eyes from both sexes and this item, therefore, appears in the general stereotype of the boy. The girls prefer black hair in their own sex, but expect fair hair in the boys in at least 50% of the cases. Both sexes tend to expect light-coloured eyes and hair in the opposite sex.

6. Tanned skin and freckled face appear as stereotype traits in the boys' descriptions and are, therefore, included in the general stereotype. The girls pay less attention to these traits in boys. The boys, however, esteem tanned skin in girls and put it third in the hierarchy, whereas girls put it at the end. It is, therefore, included in the general stereotype.

7. The boys particularly stress impoliteness in their own sex, and it comes almost at the top of the list. The girls point out their arrogance and boastfulness.

8. Only the boys find themselves as having a sense of humour, and only the girls describe the boys as cynical.

9. Only the girls mention gaiety in boys and add a nuance of rebelliousness to their aggressiveness.

10. Only the boys stress sincerity in boys.

11. The girls themselves emphasize the element of influence and status much more than the boys, who do not especially value it in the opposite sex.

12. The addition of the trait 'intelligent', 'bright and clever' in describing their own sex, is almost exclusive to the girls and in the stories it receives a nuance of the intellectual.

As stated in the former paragraph, there is a large degree of identification between the subjects and the Sabra-boy or girl. As far as there are critical remarks about 'the typical Sabra-traits' one can say:
a. Criticism grows with age, as expected.
b. There is much more criticism in the small group of 'Sabras born abroad' of both sexes than in the group of real Sabras, and here we find remarks that identify the activism of the Sabra with inner restlessness.
c. Boys are more critical of girls than girls of boys.
d. 'Sabras born abroad' of both sexes are much more critical of the Sabra-girl than of the Sabra-boy.

The last two points may appear somewhat surprising. This may, perhaps, be explained by the fact that, if the traits of aggressiveness, boastfulness and impoliteness are criticised (as unfeminine) then they are much more repellent in women than in men.

As far as generalisations can be made, it cannot be said, however, that the same reaction is present in those who came to Israel at an older age ('not real Sabras') as there, in both sexes, the behaviour of the Sabra-boys is sometimes called 'barbaric', but never in connection with Sabra-girls.

It would appear:
a. That the Sabra-girl, when she becomes somewhat older, tries not to emphasize so much the essentially masculine traits of the 'good mixer' [6].
b. People born abroad do not consider certain traits of the Sabra to be signs of virility but simply of bad manners.

The following can be said of the stories of the three other groups examined by inspection:
a. Contrary to expectation, we did not find any difference between the Kibbutz-group and group I: Not only is there no claim that 'the Kibbutznic is the real Sabra', but even in the 'staging' of the happenings the person described is not always a Kibbutznic.
b. Because of the smallness of the religious group, their stories cannot be used for any generalisation.
c. In the Teacher's Seminary (mostly girls about 22-23 years old) the stereotype, as far as it is accepted, does not differ from that of group I, except for a greater degree of self-criticism in Sabra-girls. But in

---

6. 'Chevremanit' - good mixer, with an undertone of boyishness.

this group the rejection of the stereotype, and of the assumption that there is such a thing as a typical Sabra, was especially strong - 18.5% in comparison to 0.6% in group I and this sometimes with a detailed reasoning, but sometimes also with many guilt-feelings.

5. THE SABRA: A FIGURE OF THE PRESENT OR OF THE ROMANTIC PAST? IDEOLOGICAL ELEMENTS IN THE STEREOTYPE

A few remarks about the traits brought out in the self-image of the Sabras may suffice.

From reading the stories and the survey of the hierarchical structure of the stereotyped items, it became clear that there is a problem regarding the time dimension of the stereotype figure. There is an outstanding discrepancy: Most of the persons described correspond to the age of the subjects, yet their appearance - as far as dress is concerned, e.g. the negligent simplicity (which is called in one story 'the Israeli dandyism'), sandals and 'tembel'-hat, and especially the girl in slacks, sometimes in shorts - is one no longer fancied by even a minority of students.

Hence - the ideal of yesterday is 'ideologically' binding also today and, therefore, a great number of characters are described as belonging to youth movements, while at the same time there is much criticism of the 'salon'-type (particularly of the man). There are more stories containing criticism of this kind than those in which the person described is actually a 'salon'-type (25% as against 8%).

Considering the pre-dominance of the ritualistic 'uniform' of the Sabra and also taking into consideration the almost unanimous impression of foreign visitors, it is perhaps surprising that nationalism and pioneering are relatively low in the hierarchy of traits.

Two or three factors explain this:
a. It is because the ideal of yesterday is so rigidly binding that the Sabras see in the non-fulfilment of *this* ideal a lack of proper 'nationalism', and even more of proper 'pioneering' and only 'self-fulfilment in the Kibbutz' or similar deeds are mentioned as real pioneering.
b. Taking into account the general 'active' atmosphere of the stories (and of the Sabras), nationalism is much more *implicitly* contained in the *context* of action than in the personality traits or as an ideological dimension, and this fact may explain why it is not more explicitly mentioned. (If we had used the technique of check-lists, the

element of nationalism, at least, would probably have been more prominent).
c. It is also possible that this trait is considered as self-evident and therefore not specifically mentioned.

It becomes clear from the discrepancies mentioned, and even more so from the content of the stories (the discussions which are found there, the guilt-feelings, the cynical laughter, etc.) that there is a crisis and an ideological disorientation regarding ideals and values. I would not call this a state of emptiness (of lacking ideals of which youth is loudly accused), but a crisis and an ideological vacuum of the school youth and the former members of the youth movements. It is also obvious that it is not the youth who are to blame for this but the leaders and educationalists who, with their mental rigidity and their pseudo-revolutionary conservatism, are unable to discern the social revolutions of the technological-nuclear age. In their inflexible orthodoxy, they hold up as an ideal to youth an out-dated mode of life, and all that is not 'self-realisation' in the framework of an agricultural settlement, etc., they dogmatically call 'salonic' (a very stupid expression, indeed). Youth does not find its future within the framework of these orthodox ideals and guiltily chooses the 'salonic' way... defending itself with a cynical mask against accusations of 'treason' and against their feeling of ideological disorientation.

6. DIFFERENT DIMENSIONS OF STRENGTH

It is absolutely clear that most of the traits revealed in the stereotype, directly or indirectly, concentrate on the element of 'strength' as strength and physical health, strength of character and the joy of viewing the self-image of that dynamic and complex-free figure.

Traits of strength are not only directly described by such words as: uprightness, tallness, height - or active, free, aggressive, rebellious, high status and influential, but also by words which indirectly convey the meaning of strength such as strong = without inhibitions = free... 'Inhibitions' (weakness, complexes) meaning not only all that is not straightforward (truthful, sincere) but also all that is diverse, cultured and polite. There is no doubt that we must understand the lack of politeness, the boastfulness and arrogance as a demonstration of strength (it is sometimes claimed outright that a free people in its land does not need good manners).

There is no need to point out that this exaggerated self-confidence, the noisy self-assertion, the demonstration of power, are necessarily based on the extreme lack of self-criticism and/or are an expression of over-compensated feelings of insecurity.

It seems that we must take into account both these factors. On the one hand there is lack of self-criticism, understandable in view of the attitude of the adults towards the 'idol', but there is also over-compensation; what else are the noisy demonstrations for? It seems that the insecurity is expressed in the stories by the allusion to 'shyness' which is but an expression of feelings of insecurity at the moment one leaves the familiar, limited domain.

There is also another form of over-compensation, according to the principle 'aus der Not eine Tugend zu machen', where single-mindedness and ignorance of worldly matters are presented as traits which add a special charm to the person (such as: 'The innocent Sabra in the great world').

One should, of course, also bear in mind the factor of reality, the period of the War of Independence when, like everywhere else in the world in similar circumstances (although in different ways) the significance of strength is exaggerated, and always in the direction of one's own achievements.

However, there is no doubt that the dominant traits in the self-image of the national stereotype are impoliteness, arrogance and boastfulness. Such an extreme emphasis on negative traits would point to an extreme self-criticism, and we have just doubted the existence of a self-critical attitude.

The solution to the apparent paradox is that these traits in reality are *not* considered as negative and even if not regarded as unequivocally and manifestly positive, then at least, let us say, they are indirectly approved of with an attitude of ambivalency.

There are many stories in which these traits are openly approved. In others, the impertinence is explained and justified as 'adding charm', or as a sign of freedom, existing only as an external trait, as an expression of the simplicity of manners and sincerity which is erroneously regarded as impertinence or impoliteness; or - these traits are taken to be necessary for pioneers and conquerors of the desert in line with the theory of the 'desert-generation'... and the manners of the 'Wild East'.

'He was good-hearted, but he wanted to appear tough through his impudent behaviour and self-confidence, and all this in the company of people. But when he was with only two or three friends, his impudence disappeared and he revealed himself as being shy and sensitive' -

'But, Daliah was also very sincere, and if she was somewhat impudent in her speech it was not real impudence, but a kind of truth which people did not like to hear and considered as impudence.' These examples are quite characteristic of the rationalisation and weakening of the problematic traits.

At a first glance this ambivalency towards these traits may give the impression that the Sabras struggle with the values of the adult world. It seems, however, that things are more complicated. Namely, the reaction of adults is (in the same groups, at least) not negative, but contradictory at the official, verbal level, from the inofficial, non-verbal level. Thus by the reaction of adults the child receives simultaneously contradictory communications: At the same time, when the mother says: 'You should be ashamed of yourself, is it not nice to be so cheeky to your mother?' she non-verbally (or aside) affirms: 'What a sweet, little devil, such impertinence, a real Sabra'. The child is well aware of the duality of this attitude, of the unspoken approval... because without this approval there is no doubt that impudence would not have developed as a dominant trait of 'the national identity'. [7]

7. SOCIABILITY, KIND-HEARTEDNESS AND SPIRITUAL TRAITS

The items themselves and their position in the hierarchical table do not, perhaps, always express strongly enough the extent of sociability and other directedness as hinted at in the general atmosphere of the stories.

We must take into account that not only the 'well-liked' and the influential but also the 'active' (the first of the items), and also the pioneering quality - all express sociability and the social framework of the person. This fact is still further emphasized by the contrast with the 'Diaspora Jew' who is stereotyped as unsociable and introvert.

Sociability is connected with altruism, that means, a characteristic trait of kind-heartedness which is often mentioned together with the conventional element of the symbol 'the sweet and soft inside of the prickly Sabra'.

Here it is interesting to point out that, in spite of the phenomenological agreement as to the Sabra-traits that exists between the Sabras and

---

7. This is a quotation from a newspaper following the discussion on whether education for politeness is desirable: 'The other argued that we imitate the West in so many aspects of our lives, that the only indigenous products still left were our bad manners. She believes these should be preserved as a national heritage.' ('Jerusalem Post', April 10, 1964)

the non-Sabras (although with different appraisal of some traits!) there is a radical discrepancy as to the above-mentioned item (altruism) and to the existence of a sense of humour.

In the stories written by non-Israelis, the *egoism* of the Sabra is sometimes stressed: 'not caring if she got hurt, worrying only about himself'; a point which is also expressed, although rather differently, by Sabra-girls.

It would appear that this point should not only be seen as a difference of opinion between those who belong to the Sabra-group and those belonging to an alien group, but that we are dealing here with phenomena at more than one psychological level.

We would point to at least two possibilities:
a. The elements of impoliteness, boastfulness (also aggressiveness and cynicism) may create the impression (as far as these traits are not considered as positive, belonging to a 'strong character') of disregard for one's fellow man and readiness to hurt him; that means, forms of anti-social and egoistic behaviour, which when self-criticism is lacking, are absolutely not experienced as such.
b. Sociability and altruism sometimes find expression in the readiness for self-sacrifice, for the sake of the collective (the fatherland, the gang, and sometimes a more or less anonymous collective... according to the principle that the interests of the community take precedence over those of the individual). But the same responsibility towards the individual is not felt, particularly if he does not belong to the gang.

As we have seen, intellectual traits do not play an important part, either in number or in hierarchical position, particularly for the masculine character. The discrepancy between the boys and girls' evaluation of these traits is quite remarkable: the traits 'bright and clever' which to some extent counter-balance the qualities 'stormy and aggressive', occupy second place on the girls' list and tenth or eleventh on the boys'. Furthermore, only the girls mention intelligence. Perhaps the reason for this is that the almost exclusively-valued trait in the man is strength.

8. SENSE OF HUMOUR AND CYNICISM

Although this item is mentioned last in the hierarchy, it seems necessary to dwell on it for a moment. Cynicism (mentioned only by women in relation to men) and sense of humour (mentioned explicitly only by men, in relation to themselves) are of special interest, since 'sense of humour' is the second controversial item - Sabras are convinced that they possess this trait, while foreigners often claim that they lack it altogether. [8]

This diverging opinion may stem from a semantic misunderstanding: while some understand sense of humour to mean an ability to see the reverse, humorous side of the pathetic, a gift for formulations with esprit, a readiness to laugh at *oneself*, others identify it with gaiety and robust laughter or an inclination for practical jokes at another person's expense, acts which are not necessarily regarded as humorous, but rather as roughness and even brutality.

The fact that only girls mention cynicism in regard to boys seems significant, hinting that the 'uniform' of the binding, national archetype, which is composed of elements of strength, lack of sentimentality and competitiveness precisely in the sphere of love, causes the woman and the future mother a feeling of much greater discomfort than the man. The healthy instinct of the woman reacts, at least with ambivalence towards the (obligatorily) prickly symbol of Sabrahood.

The Sabra-girl, however, accepts the axiom of the social-erotic relations where competition and conquest are more important than the expression of true feelings; where her social status grows in the eyes of her friends with the number of admirers she has 'dismissed'. But, by accepting the rules of the game 'who dismisses whom', she must accept the risk that she is the one to be jilted... and that hurts, even if she is ashamed to admit it, or what is worse - even to show that it hurts. All the same, she will call it cynicism if someone is hurt out of sheer indifference and lack of consideration by another.

It may be that this ambivalence and the as yet unresolved problem of 'what is healthy, national femininity?' are the reason why, contrary to the popular figure of 'Yisraelick', who became an almost official Sabra-symbol, the image of the Sabra-girl has not yet found a plastic expression. The muscular girl in uniform, with rough masculine movements, does not present a very aesthetic appearance, while the naked beauty with the sten-gun may indeed, have an original sex-appeal and publicity attraction, but it is rather difficult to promote her to an official symbol. The compromise, therefore, would seem to be the proud girl - wearing both uniform and make-up.

8. It is surprising that there is not one humouristic paper in Israel, while Jews in other countries have brought forth such a great number of satirical writers and have created a special folkloristic humour. The usual and not quite injustified reply to this is that this humour was based on self-abasement.

9. THE BLONDE FIGHTER AND THE SOCIOGENESIS OF THE SABRA FIGURE

There is no doubt that the preference of light-coloured eyes and hair for the 'typical Sabra' is a striking fact, especially since it so blatantly contradicts reality.

I came across this preference for the first time, with great surprise, when one of my patients, a good-looking man, already speaking fluent Hebrew when he immigrated, told me of the inferiority complex which arose in him when he came to the Kibbutz... because he was not blonde as 'the real Sabra' should be.

Already back in the twenties, Joseph Patai noted that in Palestine there was a large number of children with blonde hair and light-coloured eyes, remarking that it seemed as if Nietzsche's image of the blonde fighter was being realised. This sentence is very revealing, as it stresses even more, that we are dealing if not with an outright identification with the aggressor, then at least with a polar negation of the hostile stereotype of the Jew who is supposed to be dark and curly-haired, sad, physically weak, introvert and intellectual.

The fact that physical strength is often emphasized in minority groups who are constantly threatened and even in danger of annihilation, is quite understandable (the 'Muskeljudentum' of Nordau: Herzl's ideal - the military aristocracy of Prussia); however, here the exaggeration of the over-compensation is not only interesting, but it also indicates the latent acceptance and later the negation of the hostile stereotype. Moreover, one should note that impoliteness and impertinence are added to the physical traits of the northern 'Uebermensch' (superman), which are surely not indispensable traits of the 'blonde Krieger' or of the disciplined Prussian Junker. It may therefore be assumed that what we have here is not only the negation of a hostile stereotype, but also an identification with the aggressor... and, in this case, with the young, anti-semitic hooligan who frightened the defenceless Jews in the Ghettos of Eastern Europe...

The same Russian-Polish Jewry that created the stereotype of the Sabra saw in the young, unruly rustic 'goy' the embodiment of 'healthy humanity' (note the exclamation of admiration: 'Oh look at him, what a little devil, he is a real *shegez'*), a fatal optic distortion indeed, just as the illiterate Russian moujik was equally (and due to a similar optic fallacy) considered as the prototype of healthy people, a way of thinking that still dominates the ideological reflexes of the older Israeli ruling class.

It is quite superfluous to state that neither the primitive moujik, nor the young blonde hooligan are true symbols of 'healthy humanity' and that such a conception is a perverted reaction formation, no less pathological than the socio-psychological morbidity of the 'stereotyped' Jew of the Ghettoes.

It is said of Bialik that he proudly pointed to the fact that we already have real illiterates (others say criminals) and this is taken as an indication that we are like other people. This conviction is based on the same pathological conception of healthy humanity, and its first victims are the Sabras themselves in thinking that primitiveness is obligatory - in order to be worthy of the national archetype. Perhaps the fact that the antisemitic, hostile stereotyped image of the Jewish woman was less emphasized is also the reason why the image of the female Sabra is less archetypical, nevertheless revealing the same tendency of negation (should this be the negation of the type of the worrying Jewish mother?) involving at the same time a far-reaching masculinization of the personality, in the sense of the girl in uniform.

10. STORIES ABOUT THE 'DIASPORA JEW'

From the story: 'Chaim's Way'

The conversation was animated. Someone said: 'I would like to know Chaim's opinion.' At that moment Chaim entered and sat down. Chaim was a typical Diaspora-Jew.

Continue this sentence and describe Chaim as fully as possible.

(A girl, 15 years old)
He looked older than his age because of his clothes, which were typical of Diaspora Jews. He was an orhodox Jew, with beard and side-burns. He was very different from the others present, who were Israeli-born and his views were also different from theirs. He seemed to them strange and unusual.

Chaim was a very meek person. He was quite grown-up, never expressed his views and did not unburden himself to his friends. He had gone through a great deal in his life, had been imprisoned in concentration camps and maybe for this reason he was reticent. He always looked frightened; his eyes were piercing, expressing fear and a lack of confidence.

His hair was greying, although he was only 25 years old. When he saw a policeman, the fear in his eyes grew still greater and he would try to keep away from him and to hide, as if fearing that he would be arrested.

The memory of the camp constantly haunted him and sometimes we could see him sunk deep in thought, suddenly trembling as if remembering one of the many atrocities he had seen and suffered.

This description is taken from reality and from imagination.

From the story: The Girl-Friends

However hard she tried, she could not find a common language with Sarah. She had already known her for several months but still they were strangers. Sarah was a typical Diaspora Jewess.

Continue this sentence and describe Sarah as fully as possible.

(A girl, 16 years old)
She was a Sabra girl, with plaits down to her hips, very lively, full of song and noise. Sarah on the other hand, had short, straight hair, a sad face and sorrowful eyes which contained memories of the past. They sat together on the same bench at school. Sarah was always silent; she never spoke without being asked. Her voice sounded apologetic: it was soft and humble. Sarah never spoke rudely to her friend. She did not hurt anyone. During the breaks, she would stand alone in a corner, afraid to be seen or spoken to. Sarah was an outstanding pupil; she seemed to have been born for her studies only. Her class-mates told us that she had never attempted to become integrated in the society around her or to imitate the girls who were coquettish in their clothes and noisy in their talk. She would sit at home and read. In class she was called 'bookworm'. There were some who tried to get near to her, but with no success.

Sarah obeyed her parents; she would never say to them: 'I don't want to'. She lived with the same notions she knew from abroad: respect for and submission to grown-ups; she would frequent the society of adults. While her friends belonged to the youth movements, where they were gaily singing and dancing, she would listen to the adults' stories of their worries and troubles concerning the hardships of life and bitter fate. Sarah was older than her age. She had absorbed all the bitter and difficult elements of life. She was a young girl without youth. All this explains why they could not make friends with her and find a common language. These youngsters, so full of life and the joy of youth, who see only the positive side of life, and want to enjoy themselves, could not make friends with a young girl who was old in spirit.

11. THE STIMULUS AND THE REACTION OF THE RESPONDENTS

The stereotyped image of the Diaspora Jew(-ess) was examined through three stimuli of story completion, and the result was a *uniform* description with hardly any variation.

First, the same text that had been used in the study of the typical Sabra was given, with the variation that Chaim (Daliah) was a typical Diaspora Jew(ess). As mentioned, there were only a few stories containing the element 'influential' or 'well-liked in society'. The stereotype of the Diaspora Jew that emerged from this story was identical with that of the stimulus 'The Friends', *including his strangeness*.

The content of the second stimulus, 'The friends' was chosen in view of some illuminating experiences in every-day life as well as in our professional work when it became clear that the expression 'diasporic' or 'Diaspora Jew' was used, in the most widely differing connections, *with the intention of expressing the impossibility of communication with someone or of understanding his strange ideas;* and also as a designation for all kinds of undesirable traits. For example, a case in point is the remark of a husband who said: 'It is difficult to live with her; she has such diasporic traits' (as his wife, who was actually a Sabra was however easily offended at his derisive remarks). Or take the case of a teacher who said that he could not talk to a colleague - a new immigrant - because of his 'diasporic notions'; or the angry remark of a bus driver who, after a quarrel with a passenger, says 'You with your Diaspora education!'

In another phase of the experiment, in order to evaluate the contextual influence of the stimulus, the text of 'The Friends' was presented with the variation that 'they have already known each other for some months and were living in the same hotel in London.' We made this change in order to separate the possibly overlapping concepts of 'the new immigrant' from 'the Diaspora Jew' on the one hand; and also in case the second, undefined person is conceived as a Sabra, he would not here be 'at home', while the Diaspora Jew would be in more familiar surroundings. However, it emerged that this change of setting had only a minimum influence with a difference in the stereotype described appearing in less than 10 per cent. The Diaspora Jew continued to speak with a foreign accent, even in London; he remained a strange and miserable figure, whether his companion was an Englishman, a Sabra or from any other country. Moreover, in the majority of these stories, he is depicted as orthodox and of East European origin. We can therefore repeat, in the light of this experiment, that it is possible to use any context which contains the expression 'Diaspora Jew' without any change in the stereotype.

It is true that the stimulus of 'The Friends' contains the word 'strange', but this by no means automatically conveys also 'miserable', 'frightened' or 'lonely'. Two persons may be strange to each other if for example the one is interested in astronomy and the other in African culture; or the one is a social revolutionary and the other a keen follower of the Marathon race or a Don Juan. The first example (like other stories in the same group) proves that the elements of 'strange' and 'different' and the like also appear when the word 'strange' is not mentioned in the stimulus.

The conclusion that the associations are formed by the words 'Diaspora Jew' is self-evident.

It should be borne in mind that any Jew not living in Israel is described as a Diaspora Jew and the countries in which they live are indiscriminately grouped together as 'the Diaspora'. For example, the Israeli Broadcasting Company, Kol Israel, has a section called 'The Voice of Zion to the Diaspora'; and the education authorities a 'Department of teachers for the Diaspora.' Frequently the term 'Diaspora' is used tendentiously, instead of 'abroad', regardless of the actual social conditions in the country concerned, or the degree of adaptation or liberty of the Jews there - be it Poland, the USA, Brazil, Denmark or Tunisia for example; and irrespective of whether the Jewish communities concerned resent the expression. For example the Jews of the USA and Denmark reject the idea, since they regard these countries as their homeland.

Just because the word 'Diaspora' is attributed to all countries, the outstanding uniformity of the persons described, who are all from the Eastern European townlets of fifty years ago and more, is most significant.

In all stories (except for some of those written by Sabras born abroad or those who reject the stereotype) there is a complete non-identification with the person described (also when the partner was a non-Jew). Even if an attempt is made to give a social or historical explanation for the fact that Moshe or Sarah were miserable or unsociable, very little sympathy is felt for them.

12. THE STEREOTYPE OF THE DIASPORA JEW(ESS)

The Diaspora Jew
Appearance
1. Lean and thin
2. Strange pronunciation
3. Weak and sickly
4. Sad eyes
5. Side-burns and/or beard
6. Pale
7. (for elderly people) - signs of age: trembling; wrinkles.

Clothes
Traditional, European clothes; hat or skull-cap; dark, worn suits.

Personality
1. Closed and strange
2. Frightened and distrustful
3. Keeps himself apart (isolated)
4. Observant, religious
5. Rigid (lack of vitality and activity)
6. Lack of self-confidence
7. Quiet and modest
8. Taciturn
9. Shy and perplexed
10. Polite and obedient
11. Sad; does not enjoy himself
12. Shows signs of stress
13. Perseverance in studies
14. Engaged in spiritual matters
15. Serious and old in spirit

The Diaspora Jewess
Appearance
1. Lean and thin, or short and fat
2. Black hair
3. Sad eyes
4. Eyes: a. black; b. light-coloured
5. Strange pronunciation
6. Pale.

Clothes
Long, modest dresses; kerchief and/or wig; worn-out clothes.

Personality
1. Closed and strange
2. Frightened and distrustful
3. Taciturn
4. Keeps herself apart (isolated)
5. Observant - religious
6. Rigid (lack of vitality and activity)
7. Quiet and modest
8. Lonely
9. Sad; does not enjoy herself
10. Limited horizons (narrow-minded)
11. Conservative, especially in regard to boys
12. Obedient and polite
13. Old in spirit and serious

There are no significant differences between the stereotypes described by boys and those described by girls. The boys pay less attention to colour of hair and eyes, and tend to place greater emphasis on traces of age and suffering (wrinkles, trembling, hollow eyes). The girls do not notice any strange pronunciation in Diaspora girls.

The examination of the two stereotypes shows:

1. The most outstanding external characteristic of the Diaspora-type is thinness and a weak body. The girls are sometimes depicted as fat, which is then connected with shortness; thinness is sometimes associated with shortness and also with a tall and lean figure.
2. The male figure is also characterized by weakness and sickliness. The

absence of this trait from the female stereotype suggests a demand for strength and compactness, from the man in particular.
3. More attention is paid to the colour of hair and eyes of the woman. Her hair and eyes are decidedly black, and her complexion pale.
4. The strange pronunciation of the Diaspora Jew is more annoying to the Sabra than that of the Diaspora Jewess.
5. The element of humiliation, as well as signs of mental disturbance and premature aging are stressed much more in the male than in the female Diaspora type.
6. All the stereotyped traits of the man were more often mentioned (number of reactions). However, an exception to this proved to be the three traits ascribed to the woman only: narrow-mindedness; conservativeness and a conservative attitude towards the opposite sex, resulting from the relative discrimination against girls in traditional education. Examinees wrote as follows: 'She was used to the form of Jewish life in the Diaspora, where women did not command respect'. '...there were also some other points. Her education was so deeply rooted in her that, although she had been in this country for six years in the company of boys, she could not free herself from its fetters. Once her friend asked her about this and she answered simply: 'I was educated not to talk with boys about anything at all; one cannot be free and easy with them'.'
7. This distinction is also made concerning the intellectual field; the boys who do not take part in social activities, sports and games, find satisfaction in intellectual activities which are closed to the girls and missing in the female stereotype.
8. More sympathy with the female figure is expressed in the adjective 'lonely' which is not applied to the male stereotype.
9. Sadness, another trait arousing pity in the observer, is more prevalent among the girls. They are described as suffering passively, whereas the boys are depicted as afflicted in their very being (inferiority and humiliation) and it is precisely these traits - in spite of the awareness of what caused them - which do not awaken sympathy in the writers but rather arouse a feeling of aversion and a tendency to keep away from the afflicted and the misfortunes that go with the diasporic image.
10. The difference beween the boy and the girl is due to the difference in the effects of active and passive reactions to their cruel fate. The girl is primarily taciturn. The boy is primarily withdrawn and his taciturnity is less outstanding.
11. The boy's affliction however is far more acute. The naturally passive

girl is much less harmed, but the boy is struck in his very masculinity where confidence and activity are fundamental; he is so badly affected that he has even acquired female traits. Shyness, curiously enough, is considered as a masculine, 'archetypical' trait, whereas it is absent from the feminine stereotype, perhaps because it is such an unusual or discordant trait in the masculine image.

12. The traditional education which fits the character of the pupils reinforces the existing traits even more. The suffering produces an early maturity and seriousness in the youths. This education intentionally fosters seriousness and solemnity in those deprived of the joys of life. The boy, instead of being active and dynamic, becomes a good and diligent student, a trait which is absent from the feminine archetype, probably more because of her femininity than any deprivation in her education.

13. The politeness of the boy is also more stressed than that of the girl. All the traits shaped by education, such as: diligence, politeness, obedience and to a certain extent seriousness, are consistently negated by the writers, together with the negation and criticism of all the other traits of the diasporic mentality. It is possible that politeness and studiousness are mentioned specifically in the masculine figure, since it is he who, with all his character traits, irritates and shames the Sabra the most.

13. THE DIASPORA JEW - A FIGURE OF THE PRESENT?

The Diaspora Jew described is usually from Eastern Europe and automatically belongs to the traditionally orthodox. He is also always depicted as having experienced persecution and pogrom. Taking into consideration the age of the persons described, a historical distortion is evident here: they are in their late teens, were born after the war and could not possibly have lived through so many persecutions and abuses in their young lives. The examinees even suppose that some of those they describe had gone through the most terrible experiences in the Holocaust.

More proof of such uncritical reasoning may be found in the material. The descriptions of the Diaspora Jew's clothes, for example, are entirely unrealistic - even more so than the descriptions of the Sabra's way of dressing. The item which attracts particular attention is the traditional (religious) way of dressing: skull-cap and kaftan for men and kerchief, sometimes even a wig, for women - surely not characteristic of even a small fraction of contemporary Jewry, except in a few secluded quarters, and even then in Israel perhaps more than elsewhere.

'...Once when she took off her funny hat, we saw that she wore a wig, a black one. Her hair underneath the wig was cut short like a boy's'. And this is said of a girl - a wig on the head of an unmarried girl! Apart from the distortion of the time dimension, this is also a display of ignorance (and falsification) of the mores of traditional, East European Jewry.

All this testifies to an involuntary and perhaps subconscious transgression of the boundaries of time, place and critical judgement, into an unrealistic world in order to justify a preconceived image that does not stand up to logical analysis. The stereotype of a former generation is accepted uncritically in spite of actual knowledge, which should at least arouse some doubt.

We may find another surprising detail in the descriptions of external appearance. Previously, the Sabra girl was described as having plaits or, as the style was sometimes called 'Israeli braids'. Now some of the Diaspora girls are also granted plaits but whereas long hair on the shoulders of the Israeli girl is charming and attractive, on the shoulders of the Diaspora girl it becomes a sign of sorrow and backwardness.

In some cases the plaits of the Diaspora Jewess were a cause for scorn: 'The boys kept themselves apart, as usual... they were laughing at the long plait that fell on her back, at the pale colour of her skin which to them looked a little like 'cream'.' In other words - the same trait may be accompanied by different, contradictory feelings for different stereotypes.

It is not the trait therefore, even if it is a real one, which determines the attitude towards the figure, but the pre-existing attitude towards the figure which determines the affective 'interpretation' of all its traits; a fact which is of course characteristic for the psychology of stereotypes in general.

14. STRANGE, DIFFERENT AND AN ALIEN ELEMENT

The words 'alien and different' are repeatedly mentioned and sometimes even assume the stronger meaning of 'strange', 'peculiar', 'eccentric'. The description of the person sometimes concentrates only on the aspects of strangeness.

It is significant to note that the strangeness is automatically attributed to the Diaspora Jew and not to his partner, regardless of whether their meeting place is in Israel, London or anywhere else (according to the stimulus). The fact that strangeness appears as part of the concept of the Diaspora Jew indicates that the concept of the Diaspora Jew is not only demographical but the concretion of preconceived ideas - a stereotyped image.

In all the stories the Diaspora Jew appears as 'alien' in a certain group. His friend, on the other hand, is depicted as the representative of the group to which the Diaspora Jew formally, but not physically belongs. In most cases, even where the partner is not mentioned, the host group is explicitly discussed. The Diaspora Jew seems to belong to it only provisionally, whether this group is described as an active 'absorbing group' or as an 'adaptation group' to which the Diaspora Jew must adapt himself, or as a reference group to which he is supposed to liken himself. The strangeness in all the stories is, therefore a social-cultural trait, an essence of alienness to the group, dissimilarity from the members of the group.

Not only the 'real' Sabras but also most of the 'Sabras born abroad' stress the strangeness and difference [9], whereas only a small number of those born abroad denied the existence of a stereotype and criticized the Sabras' attitude toward the Diaspora Jew.

This attitude is expressed in the various stories by feelings of pity and a wish to help, forgiveness mixed with repulsion, a lack of understanding, sharp criticism and an unwillingness to form contacts.

Here is an example of two remarks made by German-born students who criticize the negative attitude toward 'the stranger'. '...She has problems of her own and she is not willing to take an interest in the new immigrant'. '...The Sabras concentrated on themselves and their own society, and did not look favourably on the new immigrant who had come to join them. They were strongly opposed to accepting her into their circle, although they did not know her. Sarah, envious of their games, concentrated on reading and studying but that does not help either. She became an excellent pupil, but their blind hatred turned into envy: they envied her talent and hated her. They called her 'flatterer'; Sarah remained isolated. They did not accept her; they rejected her. 'She is diasporic; she does not belong to us', they used to say.'

In many stories, we find explanations for the strangeness of the person described: historical, cultural, psychological and ideological reasons,

---

9. As one Polish-born boy wrote: 'He was different from me, different from the free, lively and gay Sabra; therefore I could not find a common language with him.'

and we have found that the rejection is strongest when based on an ideological background, when the person is seen as symbolising an anti-Zionist ideology.

15. FEAR, SECLUSION, ISOLATION AND LACK OF LIVELINESS

'Fear was one of the reasons for his seclusion and suspicions.' Fearing persecution, accompanied by scorn and contempt, the Jew kept himself isolated in his home. '...Moshe was frightened of the Gentiles. In the evenings he would sit at home, afraid to go out alone.' Because of lack of confidence in human beings, which he has acquired with the Gentiles, the Diaspora Jew closes his heart to others. The seclusion is physical as well as spiritual, the former serving to encourage the latter. 'She was withdrawn into herself and into her home.'

The exclusive devotion to Bible study enhances even further the social seclusion which was imposed under the pressure of circumstances of hardship. A life whose very essence was the study of the Bible 'has marked him and forced him into social isolation and withdrawal from other people.' Historical and social factors together therefore have produced this most outstanding trait of the Diaspora Jew - his seclusion.

The tendency to isolate oneself is a more active variation of this seclusion, both being based on lack of confidence. Moreover, the seclusion strengthens the withdrawal because, the Jew, having become accustomed to look after himself, loses interest in other people and keeps to himself. The seclusion is the result of the negation of basic civil rights: freedom of speech and movement.

'...The freedom in which he now lives was not comprehensible to him. He cannot grasp the fact that now he can speak his mind freely without fear of denunciation. In the Diaspora he was inferior to the Gentiles, and used to spend most of his time at home.'

The seclusion, resulting from the lack of freedom of speech and movement, is characterized by the absence of self-expression and free behaviour. In contrast with this, security in life assures freedom in behaviour.

'...When she came to Israel she saw a new kind of life there. She saw free, gay and happy young people, free from the shouts of contempt directed against the Jews.' The seclusion, in which freedom and self-expression are inhibited, is the basis of a lack of liveliness and social activity. Modesty and shyness are but a variation of the lack of liveliness and similarly they are also both the expression and the result of the seclusion which has made it difficult for people to form contacts with others and has thus turned them into taciturn, modest and shy people.

Fear, therefore, is at the basis of the seclusion which is characterized by the lack of liveliness and all the forms of restricted self-expression in society. The seclusion is a denial of freedom, a denial which embraces all forms of behaviour of the Diaspora Jew as he is depicted. Although the fear which is inherent in Jewish history is the origin of the seclusion and all the accompanying phenomena, it does not move the Sabras to an attitude of tolerance. On the contrary, the alleged lack of sociability of the Diaspora Jew provokes their anger and they therefore prefer to keep to their own issues 'instead of trying to make friends with the reserved and strange Moshe.'

16. POLITENESS AND OBEDIENCE

Whereas the impoliteness and impertinence of the Sabras were recognized as facts by themselves, the emotional attitude towards these traits caused some difficulties. As already mentioned, the impertinence and impoliteness of the Sabra are generally accepted not only with tolerance but even with affection. This impression is strengthened by reading the stories about the Diaspora Jew. In contrast to the Sabra, he excels in manners and obedience, and the attitude towards his manners and obedience is negative. His obedience is a cause of astonishment: '...His respect for his parents seemed peculiar and strange to his friends; he obeyed them in everything, accompanied them, came home at the fixed time he was told - not like his friends who would be late and who played in the street. His father was like a saint for him.'

Sometimes the obedience arouses opposition and rejection because it puts up a barrier to real friendship. Absolute obedience of parents interferes with the closeness and intimacy of relations between young people, who often rebel against their parents.

The politeness is primarily negated as alien [10]. It distinguishes the Diaspora youth from the Sabra. It makes them stand out as exceptional in their society: 'His outstanding courteousness, the use of so many words of politeness, widen the gulf between us.' As though it were

---

10. In many stories the demand for politeness is mentioned as characteristic of Europeans only, but actually also those who come from Iraq, Algeria and many of the African students studying here complain bitterly of the lack of good manners in Israel.

something repulsive, this politeness is the subject of ridicule: 'He did not run and play around freely in the street as we used to. He spoke seriously, in contrast to the rest of us who liked to fool around and talk nonsense. His exaggerated politeness made us laugh and then we would become aware of his origin.'

The Sabras also know how to explain their aversion for politeness. First of all, they oppose exaggerated politeness: 'Because he was educated in an atmosphere of European culture, his manners were so perfect that Ilan found them exaggerated.'

But mainly they regard politeness as artificial and an obstacle to friendly, simple and natural relations. 'She always spoke with a certain politeness and that too kept us apart. At first we thought it was hypocrisy. We are not used to culture and manners.'

Politeness is regarded as falsification, a falsification of genuine emotional expression: 'She was of course well-mannered, but these manners did not reflect her true attitude.'

And moreover, what is politeness if not a yielding to coercion imposed by authority? A curb to liberty and a blocking of free interpersonal relations? '...He was a polite boy... he was not like them, the cheeky Sabras who are free in their speech and actions.' Impertinence, impoliteness and freedom intermingle. Freedom is certainly desirable, and so are the impertinence and impoliteness that go with it. A well-mannered boy cannot be free and honest, and should therefore be rejected.

It is relevant to note in this context that non-Jews often mention 'strong family ties' as a positive trait in their descriptions of the 'stereotyped Jew'. In the stories of our group this trait was not only caricatured as showing a lack of courage to be free, but was even depicted as a particularly negative trait.

17. INTELLECTUAL TRAITS AND RELIGION

The Sabra was described as serious and reasonable; the Diaspora Jew as mature in spirit. The seriousness of the one however is not like that of the other. The seriousness of the Sabra balances his gaiety, in spite of which he can also be serious. But the seriousness of the Diaspora Jew complements his sadness. While that of the Sabra, at the right time, does not inerfere with his alertness, that of the Diaspora Jew is depicted as being contrary to liveliness. 'Moshe's fields of interest were different from those of the Sabra. The Sabras are mainly interested in active pursuits such as dancing, sport and so on. Yet Moshe is more interested in intellectual activities, reading books and collecting stamps.'

Instead of participating in games, dances, parties, the serious Diaspora boy prefers spiritual activities. He sits at home reading and preparing his lessons. But the intellectual occupations, since they contrast with the physical activities and social animations, do not arouse respect in the Israeli-born. They regard them as a substitute for social life, an escape from it: 'Most of the time she was absorbed in her reading, but this was simply a (certain) escape... Although she certainly found much pleasure in it, in serious discussion with her you could discern how much she understood of her reading, it was nevertheless an escape - an escape from the society around her into which she could not be absorbed.'

The Sabras do not appreciate the Diaspora boy's success in his studies. It is not regarded as cleverness or understanding but being merely the result of diligence and exaggerated studiousness. 'His main interest lay in his studies, in which he excelled not so much because of brains but because of diligence.' The Sabras are ready to approve of distinction in studies only as the result of a brilliant mind but by no means as the result of studying which is time-consuming and restricts a person in his social life and diminishes his liveliness.

On this point too, a hostile attitude is felt, for in the stereotypes of the non-Jews concerning the Jews, 'intelligent' is often mentioned among the first items with a clear undertone of positive evaluation. But for our subjects, even if the achievements in the sphere of learning of the Diaspora Jew are recognised, they are attributed to his diligence and not to his intellectual ability.

The religiousness of the Diaspora Jew is mentioned among the first items of the stereotype. However, it is not our task to examine the accuracy of this statement. But there is no doubt that the respondents support religiosity only in its extreme orthodox variety (in form and expression) completely disregarding religiosity as a spiritual conception, not necessarily accompanied by archaic cults and ghetto-like seclusion and totally ignoring the Jewish modernism of a great part of German and Central European Jewry in the past, and the way of life of millions of American Jews today. The figure of a reform rabbi who has had an extensive secular education, wears modern clothes and drives on the Sabbath is almost unknown to them and such a person would certainly not be considered by them as religious. It is also clear that they completely disregard the fact that nowhere in the world has extreme orthodoxy as much influence as in Israel, not only on legislation but on Jewish community life.

18. THE SOCIOGENESIS OF THE 'DIASPORA-JEW' AND THE SOCIAL-PSYCHOLOGICAL INFLUENCE OF THE TWO STEREOTYPES

A comparison of the two stereotypes which we have come to know here will bring to light, almost item by item, a complete contrast between the two figures: on the one hand we have strength, joy of life, a feeling of complete security, sociability; and on the other - weakness, fear, sadness, insecurity, humiliation and seclusion. The one figure possesses superior traits and the other inferior ones, not even arousing sympathy in its suffering. However, it is not the task of a study of stereotypes to examine the extent to which the stereotyped image corresponds to reality, the miserable caricature of the Diaspora Jew begs the question - to what extent this figure, which is described as contemporary, as an actual image, resembles the American, French, Russian or South American Jews of today. The answer is quite unequivocal - the percentage is almost nil.

It is not by chance that Israeli youth did not become acquainted with the many-faceted picture of Jewry abroad, as their educators, blinded by ideological fanaticism (here one cannot even speak of ethnocentrism but only of exclusivist local chauvinism) presented them with only two types: that of the miserable Jew who is depicted in the present stories - based on the assumption that the Jews of all countries outside Israel are virtually identical; and the healthy individual living on his own land - Israel.

Without the educational-ideological 'censorship' which tendentiously limits the obligatory literary curriculum to authors such as Feierberg, Mendele and Bialik (whose literary value we are not discussing), different conceptions might have been formed. Highly illustrative is the remark of the student who pointed out that in real life he had never met a person who resembled his concepts of the Diaspora Jew, and that in spite of his empirical experience he had formed the archetypical image that he had described. This was the result of his formal and informal education and the atmosphere and attitudes he had absorbed.

However true it may be that the Jew, living under the conditions of a minority and sometimes also a severely deprived minority, may develop over-sensitive character traits, tendencies to introversion and alienation - we must conclude that this Jew, as caricatured in the description of the stereotype, does not exist today in reality (except in a few ghettoes, some of them in Israel) but only in the imagination of hostile ideologists and propagandists.

Thus, we come to the question of sociogenesis. From those same Jews of the Second and Third Aliya (wave of immigration), who created the stereotype of the Sabra, also originated the stereotype of the Diaspora Jew. This describes the Jews of the small towns of Eastern Europe and at the same time generalises this type as if it were the only possibility.

Two mechanisms are discernable here: self-hate, or more correctly over-compensated self-hatred and a feeling of inferiority rooted in the conditions of the surroundings in which they grew up, and a denial, for ideological reasons, of the existence of Jewry of a different kind living outside Israel. (One cannot ignore the ideological overtones of the expression 'Diaspora Jewry' instead of simply 'world Jewry' or 'the Jews abroad').

Here we touch on the social-psychological aspect of the stereotype. As long as such prejudices exist, it is obvious that one cannot speak of any feeling of solidarity with world Jewry, much less of a dialogue with it. For a dialogue can be conducted only between more or less equal partners, but not if one of them is convinced that he is better than anyone else, seeing the figure opposite as a symbol of weakness and the sum total of all negative traits.

Moreover, although the stereotype of the Sabra superman, with the emphasis on exaggerated strength and self-confidence, may look somewhat grotesque, it would, in itself, not be particularly harmful psychologically, provided this uncritical attitude of superiority were not based directly on a comparison with the miserable Diaspora Jew (and the 'coward' Arab). The stereotype of the inferior 'Diaspora Jew' has an unequivocally negative influence. Without such a stereotyped pre-conception, Israeli youth certainly would not have reacted to the tragedy of millions of Jews in the Holocaust with a feeling of contempt and shame because of 'the cowardliness with which they went to their death like sheep'. (This prejudice is, perhaps, the most shocking aspect of Israeli chauvinism.)

Such a reaction was possible only because the youth was educated on a basically false conception of the world - on a mythology of heroes and cowards. Otherwise they would have known that those same heroes of the Red Army, for example, who destroyed the Nazi military machine and who, if later taken as prisoners of war, fell like dogs upon a piece of bread that was thrown into their sealed wagon after three days of hunger (as described without shame by Sholokhov in 'The Learning of Hate'); and they would have known that French prisoners of war behaved in a similar manner (Sartre: 'Death in the Soul'). They would have known that Belgian and Norwegian underground fighters, once in the concentration camps, went to their death in the same way, and that the non-Jewish deportees from Poland, France and Yugoslavia were killed in the camps in the same way, without any resistance. [11]

The originators and propagators of the national mythology who are responsible for the creation of the stereotype of the Diaspora Jew are guilty of involuntarily injecting moral insanity in the youth towards the greatest tragedy of their people.

11. Three years after the completion of this study, J. F. Steiner's controversial book 'Treblinka' appeared, raising once again the question: 'Why did they go to their death like sheep to the slaughter?' Simone de Beauvoir notes in the preface to the book: 'Parmi les prisonniers russes, les communistes inscrits, les commissaires politiques étaient mis à part et voués une extermination rapide; malgré leur préparation idéologique, et militaire, ils mirent leur courage à mourir, mais aucune résistance ne leur fut possible.' — 'Ce que n'ont pas compris les jeunes Sabras d'Israël, c'est que l'héroïsme n'est pas donné d'abord; depuis l'enfance toute leur éducation tend à le leur inculquer sous la forme du courage militaire. Les hommes de Tréblinka étaient des civils que rien n'avait préparés à affronter une mort violente, et le plus souvent atroce.'

7. A study in xenophobic associations*

* From: 'Three Studies on Prejudices in Israel', Shikpul Press, Tel Aviv, 1968.

I. A NEW TECHNIQUE FOR STUDYING ETHNOCENTRIC DISPOSITIONS: 'CONTINUED ASSOCIATION EXPLORATION' (CASE)

Introduction

The Continued Association Exploration (CASE)-Method, which is a new technique for exploring manifest and sub-manifest ethnocentric tendencies, or, more exactly, the subjective ideo-affective connotations (contexts) of some labels of primary potency, is formally an intermediate procedure between the Word Association Tests (limiting the response to the first association), and the Free Association Methods (2, 3, 4, 5). Its development was determined by two factors:

1. Our conviction that personality and attitude investigations, limiting the free expression of the examinees' ideas (arguments, motivations, etc.) - as in the check list and forced choice methods - not only yield a necessarily fragmentary image of the explored area and often conceal the sub-manifest strata of the attitudes, but that they may even suggest an erroneous motivation for the choice of a given item. The real choice may sometimes be determined by a motivation diametrically opposed to that postulated by the test constructor or forwarded by later investigators. Our investigations of stereotypes with the story-completion method (Cf. Chap. 6) convinced us even further that the 'restricting' methods nearly always distort and dim the complexity of the attitudinal context.

2. Our experiments, using the 'classical' Word Association Technique in the exploration of the reactions to some ideas with supposedly xenophobic connotations, reveal that the first association was frequently a conventional (and neutral) one; but if the subject was asked to give a second and third association to the word, the request taking him by surprise, these further associations were often strikingly different from their first emotional 'value' [1]. This seems to disprove the assumption that the first reaction of the individual, when under pressure, is an

---

1. Discussions concerning the 'meaning' and influence of the word *'goy'* originated in these experiments. While in the author's opinion this term is highly ethnocentric, hostile, derogatory and fear-evoking (and should be discarded from everyday use) some of his colleagues in a rather pathetic denial, stated that it was a purely descriptive term, since it is used in the Bible as a synonym for 'people'. True, the first associations to this stimulus were sometimes 'people' but the later ones often proved the author's point unequivocally.

uncensored one (4), or it may well be that we are dealing here with equally sincere expressions of different personality layers.

It is not necessary to stress the fact that the examinees' psychological situation during an experiment of this kind is different from that in which he is prepared to react with one single word to the stimulus as well as from that characterized by his initial readiness to give free flow to his thoughts.

Like the procedure itself, the ideational material of the responses received by asking for more than one association to the stimulus is also an intermediate product between the one-word reaction and the uncontrolled and unlimited stream of thoughts, revealing the ideo-affective context of the stimulus word. Most examinees reported, for example, that the fourth association was elicited by the third, but that the original stimulus word persisted all the time in their mind. We would have liked to call this cluster the *sphere* of the given word. Unfortunately this theory has by now more than one meaning in psychology (Messer, Schilder) so that the above mentioned term of *ideo-affective context* will be used for its designation.

Method and analysis

The CASE consists of twelve (or thirteen) stimuli. Ten (or eleven) words are of a neutral nature or have a slightly positive or negative flavour, yet without ethnocentrically critical connotations [2]. Two stimuli are labels of primary potency in the Israeli socio-cultural reality, such as 'Goy', 'Arab', 'Christian', 'Christ', 'German', etc. The subject is presented with the stimulus word and is requested to respond with the first word which springs to mind. After giving the first association he is asked to give 'another one' [3], and the procedure is continued until five associations are received to each stimulus, or until the subject indicates that he has exhausted all the ideational content.

2. As to the neutral stimuli, neither the Dutch nor the Indians played a crucial role in Jewish history, and it was therefore expected that these stimuli would be neutral, and that the comparison of the associations elicited by the name of these concrete national groups with that of the 'archetypical' hostile 'Goy' (German and Arab resp.) would reveal interesting data. In most cases analyzed up to now the Dutch, and to a smaller degree the Indians, evoked rather favourable thoughts.
3. The corresponding Hebrew word 'od', like the French 'encore' or German 'noch' does not include the word 'one' (as in English) which may make the instructions somewhat contradictory.

The record-taking rarely requires more than 15 minutes when the CASE is administered individually. The initial reaction time (IRT) to each one of the first associations, episodic or partial blockings as well as other observations are noted.

Both qualitative and quantitative analyses of the material can be performed.

a. Content analysis of the approximately sixty associations, and especially of those to the critical stimuli is carried out.
b. The average reaction time to the neutral stimuli (some of which are, of course, deeply emotionally-loaded for some subjects) is compared with that of the labels of primary potency. The occurence of prolonged reaction time, and repetition of the stimulus were rather frequent in liberal subjects, whose associations were seldom of a hostile nature, while episodic blockings (indicating the disruption of the associative process) were found among both liberal and prejudiced subjects.
c. Each association is scored from $+2$ to -2, according to its *emotional* value (EV). (Doubtful cases are scored zero - see Part II).
d. The mean emotional value score of the ten neutral stimuli is compared with that of each of the critical ones.
e. The frequency of the various associations given by a specific sample are noted. These yield interesting data concerning the *stereotypic* meaning or the conceptual 'after image' of the labels.
f. The emotional connotation of the successive associations is also noted. In some cases one finds a 'deepening' of the ideo-affective tone, in others the opposite direction is characteristic (i.e. from stronger to milder associations). We have no definite explanation yet about the mechanisms influencing the affective direction of the associative process, except that it seems that in the *manifestly* prejudiced persons the first reactions are often maximally emotionally loaded.

Two records are presented as examples. The first is of an unprejudiced, 22 year old economist, who immigrated from Poland in the fifties and is an activist of the Jewish-Arab Friendship Movement. The second one is of a highly xenophobic emotional 17 year old girl-pupil of very modest intelligence from a poor, traditional Yemenite family. (The score of the words without corresponding numbers in the record is zero. The sign V indicates partial blocking and X - total blocking).

Record No. 76 RT 9'30

IRT (sec)		Total Emotional Value (EV)
Tree 3 palm, pine-tree, apple, Palestine, box		0
Cat 2 in a bag, dog, tiger, milk, J. Tuvim		0
Curiosity 3 woman, 'the 7 sins', key-hole, science, small children		0
Dutch 5 salvage of Jews (+2), marriage with a Nazi (—2), plain, windmill, Amsterdam		0
Squirrel 5 hair, brown, snow, nuts, salt		0
Pencil 3 pen, writing, literature, erasing, old copybooks		0
Goy 5 prejudice [4], *people, religious coercion, tradition, bible*		0
Knowledge[5] 5 epistemology, Secret Service, premeditation, consciousness, research		0
Story 2 Czechov, Mrozak, Afarsejev, style, short		0
Indian 3 distant, tanned, Bnei Israel, hunger (±), Sikhs		0
Stranger [6] 5 knocks on the door, the other, Camus, coronet, xenophoby		0
Spring 3 green, rejuvenation (+1), of nations, a verse, pigeon of peace (+2)		+3
Arab 5 Khefiya, Hashemite Kingdom, Old Jerusalem, Sands, Military Government		0

EV Neutral +0,27, EV Goy 0, EV Arab 0
IRT Neutral 3,5, IRT Goy 5, IRT Arab 5

Record No. 6 RT 12'

IRT	Total EV
Tree 1 big, flourishing, beautiful (+2), nice (+1), tall	+3
Cat 2 lovely (+1), small, nice fur (+1), beautiful eyes (+2) X	+4
Curiosity 2 whisper, listening, closeness, naughty (—1) X	—1
Dutch 1 land, name, good people (+2), pleasant landscape (+1) X	+3
Squirrel 2 animal, big, white, handsome (+1) X	+1
Pencil 2 big, well sharpened, coloured, writes well, cheap	0
Goy 1 *Ruffian* (—2), *Fat* (—1), *Murderer* (—2), *Stupid* (—2) X	—7
Knowledge 3 comprehension, education, acquirement, studiousness (+2), knowledge	+2
Story 1 beautiful (+2), interesting (+1), beautiful letters (+1), suspensive (+1), very pleasant (+2)	+7
Indian 2 tall, nice (+1), people, name, nice country (+1)	+2
Spring 2 fall, beautiful (+2), pleasant to sit outdoors (+1), not warm not cold X	+3
Arab 2 *Bandit* (—2), *Frightening* (—2), *Threatening* (—2), *Tall, black* (—2)	—8

EV Neutral +2,7, EV Goy —7, EV Arab —8
IRT Neutral 1,8, IRT Goy 1, IRT Arab 2

4. Concerning the EV of 'prejudice', 'religious coercion', 'military government', etc. see part II.
5. The Hebrew word means knowledge as well as information.
6. This more or less critical stimulus is not given in all cases.

Discussion

Summing up the experience to date with the CASE technique, we can state that:
1. It proved a useful tool in the exploration of the manifest and sub-manifest ethnocentric tendencies as revealed in the ideo-affective context of some labels of primary potency in the given (sub-)culture.

2. In nearly all cases two different critical labels may be explored in the total of twelve stimuli without the interference of the halo-effect of the first stimulus. This holds as long as a space of about five to six associative items separates the critical words. To be on the safe side, the label in which one is more interested should be given first. (When examining groups, alternate forms presenting the critical stimuli in reversed order can be given to test the possible effect of the associations to the first stimulus on those given to the second). The analysis of the emotional value of the associations to the neutral stimuli suggests the possible desirability of minor changes in the order of presentation of the stimuli. The analysis of the content elicited by the critical stimuli indicates that it may be preferable to extend the quantitative span of the emotional values.

3. The CASE may be useful in throwing more light on the somewhat controversial subject of the nature of 'name calling' in children. The predominantly 'innocent' or basically hostile and rejecting connotations of these terms, as experienced by the children themselves, can be investigated.

However, it is not yet clear what is the lower age-limit to which the unmodified CASE can be applied.

4. Some theoretical and technical problems concerning this approach with younger children are still unsolved, and are now under further investigation. (The number of required associations, etc.) Some interesting observations were made, such as naming surrounding objects when the spontaneous associations were exhausted, episodic perseverance, if required to give associations with closed eyes, etc. It is still unclear why, in this case, a 'wild' confabulative reaction never occurred.

5. Transcending the specific and narrower aim of exploring xenophobic tendencies, this technique may reveal some interesting data related to the dynamics of the thought process itself - not only in children but also in adults.

6. As to the quantification of the emotional value of the items, a careful approach is recommended, based on the explicit character of the associations. For example, in spite of the fact that there are strong indications to the stimulus 'Dutch' such as 'wooden shoes' or 'windmill' have a pleasant feeling (indicating a romantic-rustic atmosphere) or 'robust' (to the stimulus 'Goy') an unpleasant one, they should preferably be given the neutral zero. Sometimes an inquiry is indispensable, as when nations are mentioned, personal names, colours and associations related to the subject's profession. A more serious limitation concerning the significance of the purely quantitative data is caused by the associations elicited according to the 'law of opposition' (e.g. to the stimulus Arab, thief, fearsome, friendly...). This type of association may sometimes be related to underlying ambivalence as well as to purely 'mechanical' causes. Yet in both cases, the mutually neutralizing scores (+2, —2) distort the significance of the numerical end results. The same is true if a definite blocking occurs and less than five associations are given.

REFERENCES

1. ALLPORT, G. W., *The Nature of Prejudice,* Addison-Wesley, 1954
2. JUNG, C. G., 'The Association Method'. *Am. Jour. Psychol.,* 1910, V, 21
3. ECDAHL, O., 'Effect of Attitude on Free Word Association', *Gen. Psychol. Monographs,* 1929, V, 5
4. STEIN, M. I., 'The Use of a Sentence Completion Test for the Diagnosis of Personality', *J. Clin. Psychol.* 1947, V, 3
5. RAPAPORT, D. - SHAFER, R., *Manual of Diagnostic Psychological Testing II,* N.Y., Macy Jr. Foundation, 1946.

II. ONE THOUSAND ASSOCIATIONS TO 'GOY' AND 'ARAB' [7]

The results of the examination of 209 [8] subjects, from 7 different groups, with the CASE technique described in Part I of this chapter[9], are presented.

7. In co-operation with Sh. Eisenberg.
8. The authors want to thank their students I. Berman, L. Brukman, T. Golberg, A. Libak, A. Spektor and O. Zucker for their participation in the study.
9. The CAsE was administered individually to all subjects except those of groups II and VI.

In the data analysis each group is handled individually and group comparisons are carried out. However, one should keep in mind what was said in the Introduction concerning the comparability of ethnic or ideological sub-groups, which is always necessarily partial, since the group can seldom be matched on all relevant variables, such as years of education, date of immigration, social status, country of origin, etc. Some of the groups are partially matched, and sometimes they partially overlap. (For example, in the groups described below, the Clinical group comprises Ss of different communities, Group I has a sub-group which could belong to group III and also some Ss who are religious, etc.) Also, the relatively small number of examinees in the respective groups prompts one to avoid generalizations.

The examined groups were:

I. *Kindergarten and primary school teachers* (N = 40, all females); Sabras and foreign born Sabras of European descent, some of whom are religious, mostly in their twenties, and comprising a sub-group of 9 Polish born Ss around their forties, who immigrated to Israel between 1930-1939.

II. *A class of 3rd-year students of psychology* (N = 25, m = 11, f = 14) predominantly Sabras and some of the older ones of Polish, German and Tunisian origin. The Emotional Value of the associations of this group was fixed by the Ss themselves and also, independently, by the authors. The correlation between the self-scores of the Ss and that of the authors was r = +0.83 for 'Goy' and r = +0.80 for 'Arab'.

III. *An East-European 'old timer' group* (N = 21, m = 11, f = 10). A random sample of subjects of Polish, Russian and Baltic descent, in their fifties, who immigrated between 1925-1935, and from various occupations and educational levels. On the whole this group has a somewhat lower educational standard than the two previous groups. Most of these Ss once belonged to Socialist-Zionist Youth Movements.

IV. *A left-wing group* (N = 39, m = 21, f = 18). Mostly Sabras and foreign-born Sabra students, some academicians and workers who immigrated from Poland in 1958. The group comprised 9 Ss from a Kibbutz of Hashomer Hazair and 30 Communists and Haolam Hazeh members or sympathizers; most of the latter being activists of the Jewish-Arab Friendship Movement. The members of this group and those of Group II are of the highest educational level.

V. *A Middle-Eastern group* (N = 19, m = 12, f = 7). Sabras and foreign-born subjects whose parents had immigrated from the Arab countries, including some older subjects who grew up in those states. The Ss follow different occupations and are of differing educational levels, and include a greater number of skilled and semi-skilled workers than in the other groups. Data of political allegiance (ranging from Herut to Mapai) are available for some.

VI. *A class of third-year pupils of a religious high school* (N = 39, m = 23, f = 16). This is the youngest group (ages 16-17). Sabras and foreign - born Sabras, half of European and half of Middle-Eastern descent, whose parents are of modest socio-economic status.

VII. *Clinical group* (N = 26, m = 14, f = 12). As from the private practice of the author and an Out-patient Clinic of the Workers' Sick Fund - thus subjects with whom the authors are well acquainted (more so than with any of the other groups). They are from different countries and occupations. Age range from 17 - 55. They belong to different nosological categories, predominantly neurotic, hypochondriac, depressive, schizoid, borderline and character disorder cases.

In comparison with the general Israeli population, the total absence of immigrants of Western and Central European origin and of the very primitive 'Orientals', the numerical under-representation of Group V as well as the over-representation of the left-wing section in our study, should be pointed out.

Characteristics of the CAsE material

Before dealing with the elicited stereo-typed images and the characteristics of the particular groups, some general remarks are pertinent:

1. Regarding the quantification of the emotional value of the associations: while in the majority of cases it seems to reveal adequately the 'general attitude' and strength of the effect evoked by the stimulus, in individual cases the limitations of the significance and meaning of the scores must clearly be stressed.

For example, the same —3 may be the sum of all five associations but also of only three or even two associations followed by blocking. In the latter case, the ensuing blocking indicates a tendency to more affectively loaded but inhibited thoughts. Also, the already mentioned associations by opposites may result in a final neutral zero, although the content of the particular associations was by no means neutral (e.g. hate, falsity, truth, good manners). Some associations had to be formally allocated 0, although they indubitably indicated a plus-minus quality due either to the ambivalent attitude ('forceful' with a coloration of admiration and fear) or the coincidence of a negative content and an attitude of compassion ('hunger', 'poverty'). In other cases, although the word *per se* was surely not 'positive', the comment of the subject clearly indicated the rejection of the xenophobic content of the stimulus ('I hate this expression', 'prejudice', 'I do not hate them'). And finally, in some cases there is a possible fluctuation not only between 0 and —2 (e.g. church, Christian) but also between +2 and —2. In self-scoring experiments both variations appeared concerning 'refugee' and 'circumcision'. (All these doubtful cases were allotted zero.) Also needless to say, in individual cases, suppression of associations should not be ruled out - as in any other personality test.

2. The associations obtained to the critical stimuli can be subdivided as follows:
a. *Descriptions* - mostly outside the figure, but sometimes also as a trait of it, nearly always nouns and (affectively) rather neutral. (Tent, church, mountain)
b. *Qualities* - nouns and adjectives, in the great majority of cases affectively-loaded. (stupid, anti-semite, educated, murderer)
c. *Exclamations* - of highest emotional coloration: 'He should perish'.
d. *Names* - personal, religious, ethnic and 'political', either neutral or emotionally loaded. (Zuabi, Jordan, Avneri, Spain, Germany)
e. *Socio-cultural and political notions* - predominantly emotionally loaded ('frontier', 'circumcision', 'Military Government', 'peace').
f. *Various* - either neutral or emotional. ('tower', 'fear')

3. The question arises quite naturally: To what extent does the CASE indicate the xenophobic disposition of the individual? Or are the associations predominantly determined by their embeddedness in the socio-cultural pattern and thus quite mechanically (re)produced. Without having a conclusive answer to that question (and, of course, both possibilities could converge) we want to state:
a. although in particular cases uncertainties should not be excluded and although xenophobic 'association-reflexes' are sometimes found to be counter-balanced by quite opposite conscious ideological attitudes, it seems to us that if *three out of five associations have a*

negative score, this may be viewed as an expression of the individual's ethnocentric dispositions.
b. Its diagnostic value is much more certain concerning groups where the significance of individual variation is reduced.

4. Similarly, concerning the Initial Reaction Time (measured in most groups by counting, so as not to increase the tension of the Ss): although in particular cases there were various types of reactions, on the whole the associations to critical stimuli were accompanied by a prolonged reaction time, as shown by Tab. I.

5. To what extent is there a correlation between the rejecting attitude towards the 'Goy' and the 'Arab'? Or are we dealing here with strictly particularized attitudes?

Here too, the relationships are not uni-dimensional and inter-individual and inter-group differences are to be noted.

There are some particular cases where very high scores on one of the stimuli, and very low ones on the other were obtained. However, in most of the very high or very low cases there seems to be a marked correlation (indicating a more generalized attitude), yet with a tendency to a more pronounced rejection of one of the two labels based (amongst others) on the dominant ideological characteristics, as well as on life experiences and on age-factor (Sabras versus East European and Middle-Eastern immigrants, etc.).

6. The neutral stimuli:
Curiosity is rather emotionally loaded and often evokes negative associations and a prolonged IRT; *Dutch* elicits at least one positive association (industrious, cultured, sympathetic), *Indian* evokes in many cases 'hunger', 'fakir', 'Ghandi' and rather often 'primitive' but also 'cultured', *Spring* equally evokes at least one positive association (love, agreeable, etc.).

Results

The quantitative aspects of the analysis are presented in Table I. The data are tabulated according to the groups, summarizing the average emotional value scores of the associations to the labels of primary potency and to the neutral stimuli, and their respective average initial reaction times (in seconds).

Table 1

Group	N.	EV Goy	EV Arab	EV Neut.	IRT Goy	IRT Arab	IRT Neut.
I. Teachers	40	—2,2	—2,3	+0,09	7,6	10,8	4,12
II. Students Psychol.	25	—1,6	—2,2	+0,10	col. examination		
III. Fourth Aliyah	21	—2,3	—2,2	—0,01	4,0	4,0	3,1
IV. Left wingers	39	—1,2	—0,8	+0,18	4,5	4,3	3,8
V. Middle Eastern	19	—1,7	—2,9	+0,50	8,4	9,2	6,6
VI. Religious High School	39	—3,4	—5,0	+0,13	col. examination		
VII. Clinical	26	—2,0	—2,0	+0,45	6,9	6,7	3,9

The stereotypical images of 'Goy' and 'Arab'

In addition to marked differences in the emotional loadedness of the ideas, there were also some striking inter-individual and inter-group differences which occurred in the associations elicited by the critical stimuli. Nevertheless the *content* of the associations and their dominant *motives* when viewing the groups as units were quite uniform.

Given this fact, and although some features of the ideo-emotional context may be absent in one of the groups, or much more emphasized in another, the data obtained may be summarized in two general stereotyped images, with the specific traits characteristic of the particular groups pointed out afterwards.

The ideo-affective context of 'Goy', according to the predominant associations (35% of the associations were negative, 60% neutral and 5% positive):

Alien-strange (foreign, of an alien creed, worships Jesus, non-Jewish, strange culture, Goy of Sabbath; sometimes as association by opposite - Jew, sacred Goy); *People* (nation, man) - *Church* (Christian, cross) - *German-Polish* (much less other nations) - *Peasant-Stupid-Drunkard* (primitive), *Educated* (elegant, good mannered), *Tall-Forceful-Robust-Joyous* (interesting, attractive, frightening) - *Blonde-hater-Antisemite* (antisemitism, ghetto, Diaspora) - *Murderer*.

The ideo-affective context of 'Arab' according to the predominant associations (42% of the associations were negative, 51% neutral and 7% positive).

Primitive (uneducated, poor, strange customs) - *Khefiya-Large Trousers-Shabriya* (tent, camel, many wives, knife, coffee); *Enemy-Hate* (murderer); *Jewish-Arab Cooperation; Egypt-Jordan* (and other Arab countries); *Neighbour-War* (War of Liberation, refugee problem, Palestine); *Nasser-Moslem-Dirty-Dark-Frightening-Coward-Friendship* (cousins); *Dishonest-Sly* ('You shouldn't trust him').

The Particular Groups

Group I. (The teachers)
1. The associations of this group are quite typical for the 'average subject' which conforms with the described model and also in relation to the intensity of the xenophobic thoughts.
2. In relation to the 'Goy', somewhat more negative associations were given by the religious Ss (stressing 'drunkard').
3. A striking feature in the associations of the Sabras is that *Goy* evokes *abstract thoughts of strangeness* (alien, etc.) of the figure, while *Arab* evokes a *concrete,* although sometimes *exotic-folkloristic* picture; the *descriptive context* (outside the figure and not related to personality-qualities) is in both cases concrete (cross, church, camel, tent) yet somewhat more frequent in connection with the Arab.
4. The transmission of the unchanged stereotype of the parents concerning 'Goy' which is revealed here, is very instructive. Sabras who had practically no contact with 'Goyim' emphasize 'drunkard' and 'tall, forceful' - although this latter element should not impress the 'sane, muscular Sabras' as one of the most outstanding traits of the foreigner, and even less should it be accompanied by an ambivalent attitude of fear, appraisal and envy. The *Nordic* character of the figure (blonde, fair) is also unambiguous - obviously the concept their parents had. This also proves that the Arab (dark) is, except in very few cases, not included in the 'Goy' archetype.

However, the emotional aura of this label is less 'intensive' for the Sabras than for their parents, and the hostility it evokes is markedly less than that elicited by the Arab, in which associations the actual *hate and enmity* (war, enmity, etc.) are often reflected. Also, the EV of the associations of the Sabras of this group to Arab is significantly

higher than that of non-Sabras, while for 'Goy', the opposite is true.
5. The relationships are different in the Polish-born sub-group: not only is the negative emotional loadedness of the 'Goy' higher than that of the Sabras, but it is twice as high as the affective aura of the Arab. The alienness of the latter is seen in a more 'apartheid' manner, as a primitive, poor, exotically interesting and hostile figure, but lacking the vividness and affective tone of immediate experience.

This statement, however, is somewhat contradicted by the results obtained in Group III (originating from the same populations) where the negative attitudes towards the Arab are not different from those towards the Goy, and in individual cases are even much more intensive.

Particular life histories seem to determine this attitude, according to - in extreme cases - whether someone's parents were killed in Russian pogroms or whether one's son was killed during the War of Liberation.

Group II. (Psychology sudents)
There are no great differences between this group and the former one, except for a milder attitude towards 'Goy'. This can be partially explained by the fact that many of these students were (or still are) teachers. While the more liberal attitude towards 'Goy' is perhaps due to the higher cultural level of the group as a whole, in relation to the Arab, the actual enmity seems to be the predominant and equalizing variable.

Group III. (The Fourth Aliya immigrants)
The Ss of this group, who do not seem to differ greatly in the general degree of xenophobia from their sons (or more exactly daughters, comprising Group I) reveal two characteristic traits:
a. The associations of church, Christian, cross, appeared in this group more often than in any other. These notions were scored 0 in all cases where there was no inquiry as to its emotional value (and in cases where the Ss were rather tense it was doubtful if the answer would have been truthful), so that the EV of Goy might be in reality higher.
b. In no other group were the inter-individual differences in responses to the two stimuli so pronounced, revealing in different Ss polarised attitudes (although there were also Ss who reacted similarly to both stimuli), a fact that may, as postulated above, be explained by the influence of personal, direct or indirect, life experiences.

Group IV. (The left-wingers)
1. As indicated by the formal results, this group is the lowest in xenophobic associations. True, nearly all of the negative associations which appeared in the other groups were also mentioned, but they occurred less frequently. Also, while in the other groups the most unprejudiced reacted with neutral-descriptive associations, here there were many positive associations (not only those 'by contrast') such as peace, friendship, etc. and again the afore-mentioned type of associations, which are not positive in themselves but indicate rejection of xenophobia, were more frequent here, such as 'prejudice', 'chauvinism', 'religious coercion', etc.
2. Negative and hostile associations were often accompanied by embarrassed, qualifying, perplexed and dissociating remarks: 'I seem to be an 'antisemite', don't I?'; 'Hate - they are generally hated, but not by me'; 'Liar, dirty: I thought about a particular friend of mine'; or 'my father used to say so'.
Ambivalence and cleavage between the conscious-ideological and spontaneous emotional (or mechanically 'reflexive') level are indicated by these remarks.
3. The more positive attitude towards the Arab than towards the Goy can be explained by the educational effort directed towards this specific sphere, in the left-wing parties as well as actual contact with Arab friends or party members. There were few 'folkloristic' associations but relatively more personal names of Arabs. 'Goy' on the other hand is outside the doctrinal preoccupations and only indirectly influenced by a vague internationalistic ideology.
4. Markedly less hostile responses were given by Communists and Haolam Hazeh members than by those of the Mapan kibbutz: however, the latter sub-group was of a lower educational level and also comprised some of the oldest examinees (belonging sociologically to Group III) who were among the highest in xenophobic associations. And also, Kibbutz membership does not automatically guarantee participation in activities for Jewish-Arab understanding.
5. It is interesting to note that in this group there were two Ss born of mixed marriages. Both associated 'me' to Goy (remarking: 'because of my mother they consider me as such'). One of them was highest in negative associations concerning 'Arab', with the qualifying remark 'I do not think so'.
Subjects from the Arab countries produced somewhat more negative associations to the stimulus 'Arab' than the others.
6. While in other groups the stimulus *stranger* (not presented in all

groups) also emerges as a more or less critical one, eliciting some negative or ambivalent thoughts (fright, curiosity, a wish to get acquainted, mystery, suspicion) but definitely less rejected than either 'Goy' or 'Arab', in this particular group, its negative emotional value is identical with the other two.

The smaller difference in IRT in response to the critical and neutral stimuli should also be noted.

Group V. (The Middle-Eastern)
The striking feature in these Ss was:
1. The 'paler' texture of the image elicited by the stimulus 'Goy' and also, in certain cases, a fusion with the notion 'Arab' (Arab as well as Christian were among the associations) so that in a few cases there was even some doubt on to which of the concepts the characteristics were attributed.
The associations of 'church, cross, blonde' did not appear here in contradistinction to the other groups. The label 'Goy' is not often used by these subjects in every-day life and as revealed by our material, it seems that it is not a label of primary potency for them but rather an adopted and only partially assimilated slang expression and is far from evoking the same hostility as that of Arab.
2. The folkloristic concretization of the Arab was not typical of this group. He does not appear here as an exotic, but rather as a 'prosaic' primitive-hostile figure, although there were some few associations relating to familiarity and expressing sympathy.
3. In this group, too, the political affiliation of most of the subjects was noted (Mapai, Rafi and Herut), but no correlation could be found between the degree of xenophobic reaction and party allegiance (due perhaps partly to the gradual disappearance of the difference between party slogans and their real policy).
4. The most marked cases of xenophobia were found among the most primitive subjects.
5. Repetitions of associations (mostly in the neutral stimuli) occurred more often than in the other groups. This and the longer IRT may suggest a relationship between educational level and the associative process.

Group VI. (The religious high school)
1. The quantitative data alone drives home the fact that this group is the highest in xenophobic thoughts, on both critical items. Furthermore, here more than in any other group, brutal and despising asso-

ciations (adjectives and nouns) were frequent, and there were very few 'descriptions'. However, before drawing conclusions about the exclusive influence of orthodox religious teaching on xenophobia, one should bear in mind that these Ss, although high school pupils, are from rather low socio-economico-cultural strata, their educational level being among the lowest in the present sample (but not lower than that of groups III and V) and that their 'emotional age' may also play a role.
2. No differences could be found among the descendants of European and 'Oriental' parents (both belonging more or less to the same occupational categories), indicating the predominant and unifying influence of the educational (in the broadest sense of the term: textbooks, the 'gang', the street, etc.) factors.
3. Associations were given in this group which appeared in no other group, such as *idol-worshipper* and *uncircumcised* (to Goy). The response 'German' was given more often than in other groups, and more hostile and insulting expressions to Arab (dirty, murderer, etc.) were used here. Also, there were many blockings, some even after one, usually extremely loaded, association (e.g. Nazi).
4. The fact that the Ss of this group from the Arab countries were markedly more xenophobic than those of Group V (of similar origin and usually less educated, many of whom belong to the generation of the parent of the present group) confirms our observation that the children of immigrants from Arab countries are unequivocally more hostile towards the Arabs than their parents, although they personally did not suffer persecution; and also (inferring from the attitude towards 'Goy') that the prevailing religious teaching and propaganda, which is influenced by the Ashkenazi orthodox attitudes of those in charge, may render the intrinsically and traditionally more tolerant 'Sephardic' Jews less tolerant. This would seem to belie the hope expressed by many writers that the numerically predominant and religiously more liberal 'Orientals' would exert their influence on the religious sphere of the country, in the direction of reducing fanaticism.
5. Although, we repeat that dogmatic religious teaching can by no means be considered as an *exclusive* factor in fostering intolerance and xenophobia, it is equally sure that its role in creating animosity towards the out-groups cannot be under-estimated. If the highly negative attitude towards the Arabs can be explained by the 'general' atmosphere and the actual political situation, the relation towards the 'Goy' (whom the Ss did not meet at all, and which, in the Orien-

tal group is not a commonly used expression) is most certainly influenced by the transmission of xenophobic concepts by teaching.
6. The fact that more than 23% of the Ss of this group associated German with Goy is instructive. While in the other groups (explicitly or by the image of the robust, joyous, drunkard and uncultured peasant) the concretization of the archetypical Goy was related to the image of the Russian and Polish villager (in a few cases - the aristocrat), here, that of the nation which was responsible for the Holocaust is evoked by the hostile label.
We have no definite explanation for this fact.

Group VII. (The clinical group)
The small number of cases in each diagnostic category does not allow any comparison to be made to the relationship of psychopathological features and prejudice, nor is it possible to assess the role of personality and pathology versus other factors in the degree of xenophobia.

Nevertheless, two statements are pertinent from the material obtained:
1. In none of the other groups was the correlation between the EV of the associations to the stimulus Goy and Arab as high as in this group suggesting the possibility that emotional dynamics *per se* play a greater role in the attitude towards the 'others'.

2. The cases with the highest EV scores, although belonging to different nosological categories, have the following traits in common: immature personalities with depressive episodes and a tendency to a desperate-misanthropic opinion about the world (also their EV was significantly negative) but simultaneously also the conviction of their own worthlessness; hating others as well as themselves, a craving for love and pessimism concerning the possibility that anybody would ever love them. In the anamnesis, contempt for at least one of the parents was noted, and episodes of (hysterical) estrangement and derealization occurred.

Thus, one can speak here about a rather generalized readiness to hate, not only others but even one's self.

Some parallellism comes to mind concerning Rokeach's finding that the Southerners were more intolerant than the Northerners not only towards Negroes but also towards the Whites, and his conclusion concerning a tendency to a misanthropic attitude in the prejudiced.

A final observation which is not directly related to the critical items manifests itself in the analysis of the material. Some stereotypes seem to be the sum total of a subject's associations (= knowledge) objectively related to a given notion. Such stereotypes, if this designation is at all correct, are very poor in their content and articulation. If the sum total of the associations (concerning remote lands or people, for example) are very dissimilar in the same social group, it is not justified to speak of a stereotype in the customary sense of the word. However, if the associations of the members of the group are similar - it is justified. We are dealing then with generalizations based on minimal information, with or *without* an emotional flavour, transmitted either by tradition or by mass media. One could even presume that, in cases where this minimal knowledge is the selected remainder of a former somewhat richer information, this remainder is either the most emotionally loaded detail (India - hunger), or a detail which is striking, according to the principle of the 'rare-zero reactions' (e.g. Turk - many wives), or that of an exclusive attribute (Dutch - wooden shoes, windmill; Australia - kangaroo).

8. Patterns of rioting in Israel *

* Paper, delivered to the Second Congress of Sociology, Tel Aviv, 1970. Also in: 'Mens en Maatschappij', 1971, nr 4, Rotterdam University Press. Also Appendix I to: G. R. Tamarin: 'The Israeli Ethnic Landscape - an extinguished Volcano?', Givatayim, 1971.

Speaking of collective violent behaviour in Israel, the most striking feature to be emphasized is the fact that during all the years of its existence there were but few cases of rioting, and except for one special category, none of them was of the severe type as to duration and casualties. The fact that only one fatal casualty is on record is persuasive enough to support the above statement.

If nonetheless, in spite of the small magnitude of the riots it seems worthwhile to analyze these occurrences, the reason therefore is the very *distinctive* character of the particular collective-violent outbursts in their positive as well as negative features [1]. Thus, the particularity of the various types of riots may enable us to draw conclusions about the social dynamics, values and prejudices in Israeli society.

The main types and distinctive features of the riots are summarized in the scheme on p. 173 and a few comments will suffice.

Before noting our comments, a few remarks concerning the attitude toward violence [2] and its legitimacy in Israel are appropriate.

One can say that despite some highly contradictory attitudinal ingredients, the basic stance towards *collective* violence is negative and condemning. In the past, when during the struggle for independence part of the Yishuv, the dissidents (being considered by the official Zionist circles as apostates and 'beyond' legitimacy) chose the way of political terrorism, only a minority supported their ideology and practice (the myth of the 'purity of our arms' was upheld in a most naive manner), and thereafter the official historiography was highly unfair in passing in silence over the role of the dissidents in the struggle for statehood and even discriminated against the fighters of those units (pension, etc.) for more than a decade.

Even concerning the more remote past, though fights of the first settlers (Hashomer, Trumpeldor, etc.) played an important role in historiography and myth, they were presented as purely defensive and there was nothing in the history of Palestinian pioneering which resembles

1. There is, for instance, a clear-cut *communal* background to the attackers in most cases (which justifies the inclusion of this survey in our text) and equally characteristic is the absence of the 'fashionable' student riots (the only case where students were involved was indeed different); the non-existence of any direct economic motivation in the anti-Arab attacks as well as the fact that none of the last mentioned cases degenerated into severe rioting (which already suggests efficient police intervention).
2. Cf. some interesting and relevant observations in F. Zweig: *Israel - The sword and harp* (London, Heinemann, 1969), especially the chapter 'Mystique of Violence'.

American pioneering accompanied with vigilant movements, lynch justice, etc., etc.

In everyday Israeli prose, although official ideals of cooperation and social justice coexist with cut-throat competition, aggressiveness, lack of courtesy and so on, physical violence is condemned. News about arbitrary police brutality during an arrest will evoke stormy protests and many a movie with scenes of violence played the world over will be interdicted by local censorship. This is all the more interesting since there exists a cult of *toughness* and *he-manship* as signs of 'healthy peoplehood'; aggressiveness of children and youth are endorsed on the same ground, and the glorification of the Army is a tenet of near scaredness.

During the mid-sixties when 'beleaguered peace' still reigned, when commenting on the high-grade militarism of Israel youth, we stated that military service is seen not through the eyes of belligerence, but as a kind of 'rite de passage' towards manhood through tough drill and as a kind of armed safari. Politico-military activism is certainly in line with the national mythology of the fearless fighter and the despise of too much deliberation as a sign of fear; however, this has but little influence on attitudes towards collective violence in non-military frames.

The fact that the right-wing formations and parties formerly advocating terrorism were near outcasts explains why they could not organize politically violent groups (except in the context of this study some small-scale episodes between 1951-1953). On the other hand, it is highly interesting that the only place where serious *institutionalized* political gangsterism (of the left, the strongmen of the Mapai bosses) existed, Haifa, was also the most liberal in Jewish-Arab relations and in the religious domain. Only for a few immigrant groups (individual) was violence [3] an accepted way to resolve issues in their former homeland, and here again in Israel, being the underdogs, they learned the fact of life that it *does* sometimes help when nothing else moves the reluctant bureaucrats.

The following observations and conclusions can be added to the details illustrated in our scheme:

1. It is almost superfluous to emphasize that in all kinds of rioting the 'hooliganistic' element may be, at least in part of the participants,

---

3. Cf. E. Marx: 'Violence by Individuals in a Development Town', *Megamot*, January, 1970.

Types of Riots

Type	I Hooliganistic disorders	II Anti-Arab mob-attacks	III Riots of religious fanatics	IV Jewish communal riots (inter-clan violence)	V 'Ad hoc' political violence	VI Arab and Druze vendettas
Perpetuated by	Teenagers of various communities	Low class young male, partly criminal. Oriental communities	Young males (seldom also elder and women) Ashkenazi	Young males, sometimes also women. Oriental communities	Various 'outcast' groups	Sometimes the whole clan, inclusive women
Magnitude	Light-medium	Medium	Light-medium	Light-medium	Light-medium (sometimes violence caused by police)	Various, sometimes severe
Directed against	Property	Persons, seldom property	Property and/or persons	Property, persons. Symbols of authority (Police, Buildings of the establishment)	'Sacred cows' of the regime	Traditional or actual enemy
Place of occurrence	Various	Mostly mixed small towns	Various, often border of orthodox quarters	Often start in slums of Oriental immigr. (in few cases Oriental Moshavim)	Relatively often Jerusalem (Knesset)	Arab and Druzian villages
Time of occurrence	Various, mostly summer			Various Pre-election weeks		Various
Intervention of police	Half-hearted	Very firm and efficient	Reluctant, often inefficient	Efficient, in few cases brutal	Sometimes very brutal	Efficient, intervention in final stages
Reaction of political authorities	Tendency to disregard	Sharply condemning	Tendency to disregard, reserved	Condemning	Sharply, 'hysterically' condemning	Disregard or condemning
Reaction of narrower community of the attackers	Partial approval and disapproval	Partial approval and disapproval	Endorsed; tacit support of religious establishment	Comprehension for motives, violence rejected	Approval	Approval
Charge, conviction	Light	Light (before 1967) Severe (after 1967)	Light, if at all	Light	Light-medium	Severe in case of homicide

stronger than the 'official' motivation. When, for instance, in the same slum-area where every Sabbath Eve for weeks wild car races using stolen cars took place, on Yom Kippur a municipal truck, carrying workers to essential maintenance work, was stoned, the 'religious fervor' of the attackers is not very convincing. The same holds true in some cases of ethnic riots (especially in Beer Sheva where no provocation, such as the prior arrest of relatives, etc., occurred). A similar 'displacement' of motivation can also be found in cases where the instigator of violence had old personal accounts to settle with his victim, as for instance when the premises of a *Jewish* café-owner employing Arabs were demolished by the rioting mob during an anti-Arab riot in Tel Aviv.

2. The distinct difference between the ethnic identification of low-class youngsters (teenagers and those in the early twenties, many with a criminal record) from 'Oriental' communities participating in collective violence against Arabs [4] (versus the East-European background of those perpetuating religious terrorism) confirms once more our observation that extreme religious (and ideological) fanaticism is the speciality of people raised in the *Shtetls* [5] and of their sons. These religious fanatics are rather indifferent towards the Arabs, upholding segregation towards them as towards all kinds of 'Goyim' (including Jewish secularists), while for reasons analyzed elsewhere the extreme anti-Arab attitudes are characteristic of the sons of immigrants from Arab countries (especially in the lower strata and in those hailing from countries where persecutions were frequent). In these same Oriental groups on the other hand, traditionalist as they may be, or violent in other walks of everyday life, high-grade tolerance concerning religious observance or non-observance of other persons is the rule [6].

---

4. We refer here primarily to anti-Arab attacks prior to 1967. As to the characteristics of the aggressors there is no substantial difference before and after the Six Day War, but at least in some cases there is a considerable difference as to the objective provocation (though *not* necessarily by those later attacked) such as the El-Fatah terrorist acts; sometimes the attacked are *not* Israeli Arabs (East Jerusalemites, etc.) and also in the post 1967 cases the charges against the rioters brought to court are according to much 'heavier paragraphs', including attempted murder.
5. Jewish parts of small towns (Städtl) in Eastern Europe (Ed.).
6. This attitude of tolerance is even more emphasized if one bears in mind the relative propensity to violence of this group, which reads in Israel (i.e. violent crimes) 1) Afro-Asians, 2) Israelis, 3) European-Americans.
The rank is reversed in cases of riots of religious fanatics; also some Americans appearing among the perpetuators of attacks on cars, etc.

True, even a not too sophisticated Orthodox person would immediately retort that since he is commanded to observe the sacred law in the *public* realm (the 'parhesia') every infringement of religious interdictions on the streets, etc., is an offensive act against him - but if aggression is defined according to common sense (i.e. *not* by theologians or experts in international law) such an argument can hardly be sustained.

3. The striking absence of a more serious or more direct economic rivalry as a motivation of anti-Arab violence (in contrast to Jewish-ethnic riots, where it plays a prominent role) can be easily explained by the *objective* situation characterizing the prevailing employment and unemployment patterns. It is highly exceptional, that in times of recession Arab minority workers would continue to hold their jobs where Jews were dismissed or that Arabs should be bosses (foremen, etc.) of Jews, or again, that any serious economic competition exists between Jewish and Arab 'enterprises'.

Occasionally in some places Jewish workers refuse to work with Arabs, explaining this by mistrust as to their loyalty, but not by a feeling of threat to their own jobs; security reasons or the fear that they may seduce Jewish girls are a common explanation. To put it briefly: Prolonged economic rivalry is non-existent [7].

4. The unexpected finding that *various* types of riots occurred in pre-election weeks could easily lead to an erroneous interpretation, namely, that the *content* of propaganda of some of the parties, or outright incitement, played a role in the outbursts. However, that is not the case. Nobody associated any type of riot with outright influence of political activists; the actions of the religious zealots were perpetuated at least partly by circles who boycott the State and the elections in particular (although they also enjoy the support, if arrested, of the more moderate Orthodox politicians). The fact that none of the 'ad-hoc-political' riots (Group V) occurred during pre-election time is significant.

What characterizes the pre-election weeks in Israel, and what probably can be considered as a precipitating factor of outbursts of collective

---

7. In one case of anti-Arab riot (in Ramle) there existed longstanding tension between Jewish and Arab taxi-drivers - accusation of supposedly voluntary homicide perpetuated through the cover-up of a traffic accident was the immediate motive and justification for the attack; and we mentioned elsewhere the words of the mayor of Dimona, that he will himself head demonstrations if Arab workers continue to come from their villages while there are unemployed Jews in his town.

violence too, is a general, somewhat carnaval-like *laxity* of the atmosphere, partly of an amorphous 'everything is permitted' style (including buying of votes), and partly of an irresponsible courting of the electorate with unfounded promises (which according to the prevailing rules of the game, the government is free to retract or otherwise to 'undo' thereafter) [8].

In our opinion it is this atmosphere of general laxity and 'suspension of order' which may explain why a significant number of riots occurred at that specific period.

5. The Jewish ethnic riots can be divided into 1) violent clashes among groups or clans of different Oriental communities in some *moshavim* [9]; 2) episodic demonstrations of the socially deprived which at some stage of the agitation get an ethnic complaint coloration; 3) the big riots of 1959 (Vaadi Salib in Haifa, Migdal Emek, Beer Sheva) and some smaller ones in 1963 and 1965 (Beer Sheva, Ashdod) which from the beginning were protesting against alleged ethnic discriminations and where the social pattern (inadequate housing, insufficient employment at relief work, etc.) played a dominant role.

The first category is of small significance, mostly it centered around the fight for power and privileges held by clans in moshavim (that of the treasurer, of the grocery-holder, etc.) and clashes occurred between clans of the same community as well as on an inter-ethnic level.

The small-scale riots of the second type (which at the beginning of the protest demonstrations were not associated with any ethnic pattern) are already illustrative of the basic features of all the ethnic riots:

a. A fundamental intermingling of complaints of ethnic and economic discrimination. The 'non-class-consciousness' character of the protests is striking, as articulate political or socio-economic demands are seldom put forward. This emphasises the non-existence of a genuine local leadership and also the failure of left-wing parties to gain audience and to develop class-conscious attitudes at this rather chauvinistic *Lumpenproletariat*. To put it more exactly: the official left-wing parties (nomin-

---

8. Amnesty is granted to some prisoners in order to buy the votes of their clan. One closes the eyes to irregularities and a two-way blackmailing takes place; illegal pressure of public representatives on employees on the one hand, and reactions like 'If you don't arrange for my son to be admitted to *that* school, I will not vote for your party', so that many of the precepts of orderly and lawly behaviour are somewhat temporarily suspended.
9. Agricultural settlements (Ed.).

ally labour-movements) *are* the establishment, and the local 'professional Sepharadim' their docile executives.

b. The riots are the exclusive responsibility of the 'Oriental' communities (there have never been clashes against them, or between Oriental and non-Oriental communities) protesting discrimination ('dofkim et ha Sepharadim'); the slogan 'Awaken Sepharadim' appears. But even if curses against Ashkenazim are professed, the attack is never directed against any concrete 'Ashkenazi' target (political leader, specific subgroup, etc.). The address of the attack is clearly the *establishment* (or very seldom rich quarters), and in the big riots of 1959, simultaneously with voicing the ethnic complaint, the attacks were directed against the State, the police, Mapai and the Histadruth.

The 1959 riots were more unambiguous in their origins, but not much more articulate concerning the demands; though more and *equally distributed work* and *better housing* conditions were recurrent themes, as well as the complaint of discrimination in this field by the Jewish Agency and the Histadruth in favor of the Rumanian and Polish immigrants[10]. That at least part of these complaints was fully justified is an undeniable fact, as well as the generally arrogant attitude of a sizable section of the 'Ashkenazi population' [11].

It is difficult to ascertain what was exactly the role of the example of the local strongmen in the configuration of elements which led Haifa to the first mass-outburst on an ethnic basis, which probably served as an example for other places. It is sociologically interesting, however, that during the eleven years which have passed since those events, nobody has even mentioned the possibility that the legalized gangsterism of the Hapoel-commandos (in the service of Mapai) could have served as an example for the illegal violence perpetuated by the underdogs.

The Jewish ethnic riots, especially Vaadi Salib, deeply shocked the public at large, as well as the authorities. Though the ruling party did its best to present the riot in Vaadi Salib solely as an act of misled young hotheads incited by irresponsible inimical elements, and attempt-

---

10. Incomparably more arbitrariness, corruption and nepotism characterize the institutions of the Histadruth (which previously owned also the Labor Exchange Bureau) and of the Jewish Agency (on whom the immigrants depend for almost everything) than the governmental services supervised by the State Comptroller and subject to the intervention of the High Court of Justice.
11. On the theme of Ashkenazi arrogance (in the context of Vaadi Salib) see U. Avneri in an editorial in 'Haolam Haze', and some years later relating to the problem in a general way, E. Elyachir: 'Danger: Jewish Racialism'.

ed to prevent discussion about ethnic discrimination and the policy of immigration absorption, an Inquiry Committee was set up, one scientific paper [12] undertook to outline the sociological characteristics of Moroccan Jewry before and after their immigration (disproving some of the ingrained preconceived ideas about this community, but refraining from analyzing the riots themselves), the newspapers dwelt on this subject for many weeks, and serious action was undertaken to improve the lot of the underprivileged, especially in the field of housing and social care.

6. No doubt, once a riot is set into motion, it is the behaviour of the police which is perhaps the most important single factor determining its subsequent development and outcome. (The extensive American literature about riots supports this theory). The degree of professional competence or incompetence (in the sense of neither 'overcontrol' nor 'undercontrol') which of course apart from purely technical competence depends also on the directives of the *political* authorities, is crucial for the relatively quick termination of the outbursts or their possible degeneration into bloody massacres [13].

Similar to the action of the police was the categorically condemnatory attitude of the authorities, including the highest echelons, and of the press (though according to particular ideological orientation the reasons forwarded as an explanation for the occurrences and the severity of condemnation varied considerably). Thus the rioting youngsters, many of them belonging to the underworld, could by no means indulge in the feeling of having tacit approval nor the feeling of 'heroes' defending the 'true' group norms.

The condemning attitude of the authorities (and of the press) mirrors not only a pragmatic approach on the part of the political decision-makers, anxious to prevent degradation in a field which could become highly explosive, but is also sincerely in line with the value system of the overwhelming majority of the Jewish population at large. Anti-Arab as it may be in its sentiments, preferring practical segregation to any con-

---

12. Cf. R. Bar Yosef: 'The Moroccans' (Molad, July, 1959 - Hebrew text) and numerous articles of A. Nesher in Ha'aretz in the following years dealing with the rehabilitation of slum-dwellers.

13. More or less as a curiosity, illustrating the extreme sensibility of rioters interpreting (rightly or wrongly) police behaviour, we should mention the words of a participant in the riot following the first El Fatah attack on the Central Bus Station in Tel Aviv: 'The fact that the police intervened without using sticks meant that we are permitted to beat up the Arabs, only not to cause severe injury or use weapons'.

tact, physical maltreatment of the minority goes against all its norms and ideals... and against its official self-image as a democratic society.

On the whole, results prove that police did handle technically adequately (no 'over-' and no 'undercontrol') the big riots. The suggestion of some younger officers 'to use a heavy hand against the Orientals, who understand only force', which evoked a wide furor in Oriental circles, was rejected by the responsible echelons. Although a relatively large number of people (demonstrators and police) were wounded and many arrested no fatal casualties occurred and there were few cases of police brutality reported.

In contrast to the unanimous condemnation of the anti-Arab attacks, reactions to the ethnic riots were different. Although there was no verbal endorsement of the outbursts, symptoms of comprehension as well as widespread bitterness (suffering) and discrimination were perceived through readers' letters. This was true for large sections of the non-Ashkenazi population; on the other hand some of the letters reflect gross prejudices against 'the primitives who misuse democratic liberties.'

Taking into consideration the efficient intervention, revealing high professional competence, of the police in the previous cases, the more striking becomes its under-control, lack of efficiency and often manifest bias (as to the treatment of protestors *against* religious coercion) when dealing with violence of Orthodox fanatics and especially if the mob attack is *not* directed against Christian institutions... when diplomatic complications may ensue.

The directives of the political establishment to the police, one can safely infer, reveal, firstly, the attitude of the secular rulers (who in their coalitionary dealings so easily sold out civil rights to the Orthodox) not to anger the coalition partners, and secondly, that even the moderate circles of the religious establishment, who do not openly endorse the attacks (or do so only half-heartedly) would raise hell if Jewish police 'maltreated' believers who obey the command of their precepts to impose respect of religious law, or are engaged in their even more sacred duty of fighting the 'danger of missionarism'.

The majority of secular officials and also of the press tend to underplay or outrightly to disregard the collective violence of the zealots; and if the religious establishment does not openly encourage religious terrorism and only pleads for understanding, the more radical segments of Orthodoxy (also those holding official posts) and their press do [14].

---

14. Cf. our 'Forms and Foundations of Israeli Theocracy', Shikpul Press, Tel Aviv, 1968.

The rather half-hearted intervention of police in cases of hooliganistic attacks by groups of youngsters, can possibly be explained by the persistence of tenets of local mythology, considering aggressiveness and lack of discipline of youngsters as an embodiment of 'uninhibited, healthy humanity', refusing to acknowledge signs of waywardness and criminality and reluctant to intervene with the freedom to express the joy of life of free youth in their free land [15].

This brings into an even sharper light the attitude of the police and those who give the directions, concerning the rather heterogeneous fifth category, which *faute de mieux* we named violence on an *ad hoc* political background. (Ad hoc - since it is centered around an isolated topic, sometimes unconnected with the general political line, sometimes one also deals with ad hoc groups). Apart from the brutality of police intervention, which is in some cases what lends the violent element to the manifestations, such as the heavy-handed dealing of zealot conspirators [16] and the mob protesting against the reparations agreement with Germany, or of striking Communist-led sailors, of Jerusalem students voicing protest against Adenauer's visit to their campus, of Haolam Haze marchers near Netanyia, expressing solidarity with attacked Arabs of the nearby villages, of anti-Histadruth First of May demonstrators in Ashdod or anti-annexationist demonstrations in Jerusalem and its surroundings - the common element characterizing these groups is precisely that one deals with extremely *heterogeneous,* often ad hoc formations, which are all of them somehow outcasts of the national body, offending some of the 'sacred cows' of the establishment, which represents the majority of the 'honest Israelis'. This includes here an attitude of the ruling stratum: to criticise the government's wisdom in those matters is to question the very fundamentals of the State, or to declare that the Histadruth-bureaucracy is *not* an honest and exclusive representative of the workers is sacrilege.

The endorsement or even encouragement of police brutality towards

15. (We do not think that there is much truth in the explanation sometimes forwarded, stressing the 'Oriental' descent of both the majority of the rank and file of the police forces and of the rioting youngsters of the peripheries and street-corner gangs).

16. Though the acts of the zealot-underground were in essence not dissimilar from those characterizing Group III, here one deals with outright *political* violence, since they were part of a conspiracy, when an underground organization attempted to establish by way of terror a theocratic rule. One can discern nuclei of *clerofascist* organizations, for instance already in the Orthodox branch of the LHI, in the undergrounds of 1951 and 1953, and actually in a segment of the Greater Israel Movement.

the 'out-casts' (right or left groups who reject some of the fundamentals of the Zionist establishment and the prevailing rules of games of legitimacy) expresses an attitude of the establishment and the public, considering those 'out-casts' to be outside the category of 'honest citizens' and beyond the measure of acceptable opposition to which democrats have to subscribe. It reflects an attitude identifying tolerance (which is not a value in itself) with 'limited pluralism' [17] out of necessity to compromise, but no obligation of tolerance exists towards 'illegitimate' groups who reject some of the fundamentals [18]. The discrepancy between the energetic and efficient intervention of the police in crushing the anti-Arab mobs and the very lenient punishment of only a few of the participants is striking, while others were freed on the same day or the day after without being charged. There seems to be one apparent reason for this, and another which is less evident.

Given the high standard of Israeli judiciary, one can assume that the rioters would get much heavier sentences if they appeared before the judge according to other paragraphs. This however does not depend on the court but on the political authorities (Ministry of Justice, police, etc.).

There seems to be a clear enough tendency, after demonstrating the mighty fist to the mob and making it understood that every attempt on their part to take the law into their own hands will be prevented, to appease the transgressors (and/or their community) and to forget the whole episode as soon as possible. Thus, only few among the most violent will be accused with relatively insignificant charges (even if the victims were induced to plead for their liberation, as a 'gesture of goodwill') - and demands to nominate a parliamentary inquiry committee to

17. Concerning this 'to every legitimate body its share' and 'no rights to the illegitimate' type of tolerance and pluralistic democracy, see Robert P. Wolff: 'Beyond Tolerance' in *A Critic of Pure Tolerance,* Beacon Press, Boston.
18. In Israel they are the groups rejecting the rules of the games of the 'organized Yishuv', established decades ago when the present establishment took over the control of the funds in pre-State days, by a coalitionary agreement, while 'honest people' and acceptable degree of opposition mean in this context: those Zionists who are at least potentially possible partners of a coalition. Shortly after the establishment of the State the non-Zionist (even anti-Zionist in its large segments) Orthodoxy was coopted to the legitimate body, but it was only in 1967 when also the geruth heretics became acceptable. More complicated is the attitude towards the Communists. The unambiguously *demonological* image preceding the sixties (the before mentioned sailors' strike was crushed with the help of strikebreakers belonging to Hashomer Hazair kibbutzim) was, following the split of the Communist Party, replaced with that of the 'good' (pro-Israeli) and 'bad' (supporting Arab chauvinism) Communists.

investigate the sources, put forward by the press and MK's, were disregarded.

The reason for the attitude of the authorities seems to be overdetermined. While on the one hand a deep shock is felt following the pogromistic outbursts, the establishment seems to be reluctant to anger an unstable social stratum which anyhow feels frustrated and discriminated. However, the tendency to let things be forgotten as quickly as possible converges with a much more generalized pattern of the establishment and its rules of the game, when facing unpleasant phenomena... simply to suppress evidence by concealing the findings which would point to the truth - contrary to official theses and illusions. The readiness to conceal the unpleasant report is almost a reflex, regardless of whether one deals with a scientific finding proving that, contrary to official statements, wide segments of the population live below the poverty line, or a report disclosing the incompetence and malpractice in a Histadruth enterprise or again relating to explosive ethnic problems.

This is the reason why in most types of riots charges are relatively light, excepting some cases of the ad hoc political category and vendettas in Arab and Druze villages if homicidal acts were committed. Given the small magnitude of the riots, and a short term policy this tendency to avoid facing problems does work. However, taking a far-sighted viewpoint this approach was proved to be a dangerous fallacy.

9. The influence of ethnic and religious prejudice on moral judgment *

* IPA paper, Tel Aviv 1963. Also in 'New Out-Look', Tel Aviv, 1966. Also in: 'Research on Patterns of Tolerance and Intolerance', Shikpul Press, Tel Aviv, 1969.

I. The present study investigates the effect of chauvinism on moral judgment from the following aspects:
a. The presence of prejudices in the ideology of the youth.
b. The effect of uncritical teaching of the Bible on the propensity for forming prejudices (particularly the notion of the 'chosen people', the superiority of the monotheistic religion, and the study of acts of genocide by biblical heroes.

We have selected the most extreme form of prejudice: the extermination of the out-group. We asked the pupils, in direct confrontation, to comment on the following text:

G-Form-1. You are well acquainted with the following passages of the Book of Joshua: 'So the people shouted when the priests blew with the trumpets: and it came to pass, when the people heard the sound of the trumpet, and the people shouted with a great shout, that the wall fell down flat, so that the people went up into the city, every man straight before him, and they took the city. And they utterly destroyed all that was in the city, both man and woman, young and old, and ox, and sheep, and ass, with the edge of the sword' (VI, 20, 21). 'And that day Joshua took Makkedah, and smote it with the edge of the sword, and the king thereof he utterly destroyed, them, and all the souls that were therein; he let none remain: and he did unto the king of Makkedah as he did unto the king of Jericho. Then Joshua passed from Makkedah, and all Israel with him, unto Libnah, and finaly against Libnah. And the Lord delivered Lachish into the hand of Israel, which took it on the second day, and smote it with the edge of the sword, and all the souls that were therein, according to all that he had done in Libnah' (X, 28-32).

Please answer the following two questions:
1. Do you think Joshua and the Israelites acted rightly or not? Explain why you think as you do.
2. Suppose that the Israeli Army conquers an Arab village in battle. Do you think it would be good or bad to act towards the inhabitants as Joshua did towards the people of Jericho and Makkedah? Explain why.

Joshua's genocide is not the only one of its type mentioned in the Bible. We selected this particular example because of the special position the Book of Joshua has in the educational system, both as national history and as one of the cornerstones of a modern national mythology, with such concepts as 'the generation of the desert', etc.
    As an additional exploration of the influence of ethnocentrism on moral judgment, another (control) group was presented with the G-Form-2 text. This group consisted of two sub-groups, parallel classes of

the 7th and 8th grades of another Tel Aviv school (N = 168; 86 boys, 82 girls). The first sub-group was presented with the above-mentioned biblical text (asking only the first question), and the second group with a text analogous to Joshua, but presented in a 'Chinese version':

The story of General Lin

General Lin, who founded the Chinese Kingdom 3000 years ago, went to war with his army to conquer a land. They came to some great cities with high walls and strong fortresses. The Chinese War-God appeared to General Lin in his dream and promised him victory, ordering him to kill all living souls in the cities, because those people belonged to other religions. General Lin and his soldiers took the towns and utterly destroyed all that was therein, both man and woman, young and old, and ox, and sheep, and ass, with the edge of the sword. After destroying the cities, they continued on their way, conquering many countries.

Please answer the question: Do you think that General Lin and his soldiers acted rightly or not? Explain why.

We administered the G-Form-1 to nine groups of pupils, ranging from 8½ to 14 years of age, and from the 4th to the 8th grade (N = 1066, boys 563, girls 503). As we have said, G-Form-2 was administered to 7th and 8th graders in one school. The following is a list of the schools and the number of students tested in each:
1. An elementary school in Tel Aviv-Jaffa, N = 153.
2. An elementary school in Tel Aviv-Jaffa, N = 442.
3. An elementary school in a 'Moshava' (agricultural village) in the neighborhood of Ramle, N = 110.
4. A religious elementary school in the same village as No. 3; N = 41.
5. An elementary school in a small city in the Sharon: N = 165.
6. An elementary school in a well-established kibbutz in the Jezreel Valley (belonging to the Kibbutz Meuchad moderate left-wing movement); N = 46.
7. An elementary school in a kibbutz in the Jezreel Valley (belonging to the Kibbutz Artzi radical left-wing movement); N = 49.
8. A youth center belonging to a school on the outskirts of Tel Aviv (mostly deprived children); N = 45.
9. A heterogeneous group from different schools; N = 37.

Form G-2 was administered in an elementary school in north Tel Aviv; N = 168.

Some notes on the comparability of the groups are in order. Although the range of all the tested pupils fell between the 4th and 8th grades [1], it was impossible to administer the test to grade 4 in group 3, since their ability to write was so poor that we had to start with the 5th graders. Also, in group 4 we have only boys since the teachers agreed to conduct the survey only among the boys and not among the girls. In the kibbutzim whole grades are sometimes missing and in the higher grades there are sometimes children from outside the kibbutz. The statistical analysis handles the smaller groups by clustering all subjects only according to sex and not age.

II. The answers were classified in the following way: 'A' represents total approval, 'B' represents partial approval or disapproval, 'C' represents total disapproval, and 'X' represents confused or irrelevant responses (which were eliminated from the statistical calculations). [2]

'C' classification was accorded to all answers formally rejecting genocide, either on ethical or utilitarian grounds. This does not mean that all 'C' responses reveal non-discriminatory attitudes. For example, one girl criticised Joshua's act, stating that 'the Sons of Israel learned many bad things from the Goyim'. It is more difficult, psychologically, to understand her friend, who rejects Joshua's act because 'It is written in the Bible, "Don't kill"', yet, at the same time approves the act in the second question, stating, 'I think it would be good, as we want our enemies to fall into our hands, enlarge our frontiers, and kill the Arabs as Joshua did.' Another extremely racist response is that of a 10 year old girl disapproving the act, stating, 'I think it is not good, since the Arabs are impure and if one enters an impure land one will also become impure and share their curse.'

III. The results of G-Form-2 are as presented in Table I.

An analysis of the answers reveals the following:

1. The striking difference in the approval of the genocide by Joshua (A-60%, B-20%, C-20%), as compared to that of General Lin, leader of an out-group (A-7%, B-18%, C-75% on G-Form-2), unequivocally proves the influence of chauvinism and nationalist-religious prejudices on moral judgment;

1. The 4th grade is the first grade in which the Book of Joshua is taught. The 8th is the last in the Israeli elementary school system.
2. The difference in percentages of 'X' responses between the first and second question, as well as differences among the sub-groups, caused some minor but insignificant distortions in the statistical computation.

Table I. The results, tabulated according to age and sex

	Boys		'G' Form I.—%		Girls		
Grade	Question1	Question2	Question1	Question2			
	A B C	A B C	A B C	A B C	N=1066 (563; 503)		
4	93 7 0	36 28 36	63 0 37	50 17 33	I.	N=153 (76; 77); %X-13
5	87 13 0	10 20 70	64 27 9	67 11 22		
6	73 0 27	20 7 73	64 21 15	10 10 80		
7	100 0 0	7 20 73	82 9 9	35 18 47		
8	93 7 0	14 7 79	75 8 17	8 9 83		
4	74 3 23	58 3 39	77 3 20	72 4 24	II.	N=422 (198; 224); %X-18
5	90 0 10	55 0 45	93 2 5	59 0 41		
6	32 5 63	10 0 90	26 18 56	21 3 76		
7	62 18 20	18 21 61	54 7 39	18 6 76		
ë	77 9 14	6 10 84	53 14 33	12 12 76		
5	78 0 22	74 0 26	66 7 27	37 18 45	III.	N=110 (52; 58); %X-19
6	75 0 25	36 7 57	50 0 50	40 0 60		
7	43 21 36	9 18 73	47 6 47	45 0 55		
8	89 11 0	25 12 63	45 0 55	58 34 8		
4—8	95 5 0	50 3 47	/ / /	/ / /	IV.	N=41 (41; 0); %X-19
4	91 0 9	75 0 25	76 6 18	67 0 33	V.	N=165 (89; 76); %X-15
5	94 6 0	43 7 50	91 0 9	71 0 29		
6	36 7 57	0 8 92	73 0 27	21 0 79		
7	88 6 6	22 11 67	55 25 20	21 16 63		
8	56 19 25	13 13 74	79 0 21	13 0 87		
4—8	38 16 46	4 8 88	11 22 67	0 21 79	VI.	N=46 (27; 19); %X-8
6, 7	27 15 58	6 3 91	53 0 47	6 12 82	VII.	N=49 (33; 16); %X-2
4—8	84 0 16	41 0 59	69 8 23	55 0 45	VIII.	N=45 (28; 17); %X-24
4—8	63 16 21	29 6 65	50 14 36	27 0 73	IX.	N=37 (21; 16); %X-18
ε	71 8 21	30 6 64	61 9 30	34 9 58	N=1066 (563; 503); %X-17	

	G Form I				G Form II		
1.	A 66	B 8	C 26	1.	A 60	B 20	C 20
2.	A 30	B 8	C 62	2.	A 7	B 18	C 75

188

2. The answers to G-Form-1 (A-66%, B-8%, C-26% to the first question and A-30%, B-8%, C-62%, to the second), indicate the existence of a highly prejudiced attitude among a considerable number of the respondents, despite some differences in the nuances of the responses, justifying the discriminatory tendencies (religious, racial-nationalist, strategic justification of the extermination, etc.);

3. The uncritical teaching of the Bible - to students too young - even if not taught explicitly as a sacred text, but as national history or in a quasi-neutral atmosphere concerning the real or mythological character of its content, no doubt profoundly affects the genesis of prejudices (at least as a disposition) even among non-religious students, in accentuating the negative-hostile characters of the strangers (idol-worshippers, etc.);

4. The overestimation of statehood as a supreme value and the idea that assimilation is the greatest evil, and the influences of militaristic values in ideological education, are further sources of discriminatory tendencies;

5. There are some indications that in 5-7% of the examinees individual personality traits may be the dominant factor in their 'A'-answers (similarly this same percentage appears in affirming General Lin's genocide, and in the 'A'-answers to the second question on G-Form-1 in the kibbutz schools and a very progressive secondary school in Tel Aviv), while in the remaining 25% it seems to be due to the influence of the environment;

6. The inter-relationship of the different forms and roots of discriminatory tendencies (note the reasons for the differing or converging answers to the first and second question on G-Form-1; there were even some 'C' answers to the first question and 'A' to the second) presents a complex problem to be more fully investigated;

7. As expected, the overt form of extreme prejudice appears less in more cultivated areas (the percentage of the 'X' answers may be one of the criteria) and decreases with age; however, one often finds an interesting increase in the 7th grade, when the students are learning the Book cf Joshua for the second time;

8. Contrary to our expectation, there was no difference, concerning this most cruel form of prejudice, between male and female examinees;

9. A difference can be observed between the students of the kibbutz schools and other groups.

This material is a severe indictment against our educational system, against all those who knowingly or unknowingly serve as a tool for education towards intolerance, chauvinism and prejudice. It should serve as a danger signal for all those concerned directly or indirectly with education. It is necessary and urgent to bring about radical changes in the curriculum itself as well as in the attitude toward the material studied. We hope that the data presented here may help those responsible for Israeli education to draw the necessary conclusions.

EPILOGUE

Aftermath of a research

The Committee had the impression that Dr. Tamarin's research in the field of education caused harm to the relationship between the Departments of Psychology and Education and the Ministry of Education. Point 5 of the Yortner Committee's Secret Report.

The publication of this research brought it totally (at least by the author) unexpected fame... in many senses. If numerous quotations by professionals was any reason for a feeling of satisfaction, the utterly non-scientific and sometimes outrightly scandalous aspects of what was later called 'The Tamarin Affair' was a not very pleasant issue. As I stated in my correspondence with the senate of the Tel Aviv University - who was conducting my case - I never dreamt that I would become the last victim of Joshua's conquest of Jericho...

Publications of the Polemological Centre of the Free University of Brussels (VUB). *Vol. 1*

Sociology, War and Disarmament
Studies in Peace Research

Johan Niezing

If one is to solve social problems one must first get to grips with them. This applies also to the most basic problem confronting man with: that of war and peace. From this point of view there is no sphere of study so meaningful to the social scientist as that of peace research. Moreover, peace research is also admirably suited to the interdisciplinary approach. This book subjects several chapters of peace research to a theoretical analysis. Attitudes towards war, peace, armament and disarmament, structural friction within diplomatic organizations, the functioning of UN peacekeeping forces, and problems of security policy are all spotlighted. The views put forward are not only those of modern sociology, but also views derived from social psychology and political science. This book may therefore be regarded both as a fundamental contribution towards the progress of peace research as an interdisciplinary field of investigation and, indirectly, as a social scientist's effort towards the solution of the crual problem of war and peace.
Second impression

Rotterdam University Press